GLOB

CW00741465

# The best of
# BUDAPEST

## BRIAN RICHARDS

NEW
HOLLAND

# GLOBETROTTER™

First edition published in 2007
by New Holland Publishers (UK) Ltd
London • Cape Town • Sydney • Auckland

10 9 8 7 6 5 4 3 2 1

website: www.newhollandpublishers.com

Garfield House, 86 Edgware Road
London W2 2EA
United Kingdom

80 McKenzie Street
Cape Town 8001
South Africa

14 Aquatic Drive
Frenchs Forest, NSW 2086
Australia

218 Lake Road
Northcote, Auckland
New Zealand

Distributed in the USA by
The Globe Pequot Press, Connecticut

ISBN 978 1 84537 449 5

**Publishing Manager:** Thea Grobbelaar
**DTP Cartographic Manager:** Genené Hart
**Editor:** Thea Grobbelaar
**Designer:** Nicole Bannister
**Cartographer:** Tanja Spinola
**Picture Researcher:** Shavonne Govender

Reproduction by Resolution (Cape Town)
Printed and bound by Times Offset (M) Sdn. Bhd.,
Malaysia.

Although every effort has been made to ensure
that this guide is up to date and current at time
of going to print, the Publisher accepts no
responsibility or liability for any loss, injury or
inconvenience incurred by readers or travellers
using this guide.

**Photographic Credits:**
**Peter Baker/International Photobank:** pages
36, 61, 73; **Jeanetta Baker/International
Photobank:** pages 43, 44, 46, 49, 50 (bottom);
**Jon Arnold/jonarnoldimages.com:** pages 30,
35, 38, 75; **Walter Bibikow/jonarnold
images.com:** pages 31, 40; **Gavin Hellier/
jonarnoldimages.com:** title page; **Doug
Pearson/jonarnoldimages.com:** pages 32, 77;
**Robin McKelvie:** pages 41, 72; **F1 Online/
Photo Access:** page 23; **Giovanni Simeone/
4cornersimages.com/Photo Access:** cover;
**SIME/Photo Access:** page 82; **Picture Colour
Library:** pages 17, 39, 42, 45, 48, 50 (top), 52
(left), 53, 60, 64, 74; **Brian Richards:** pages 8,
9, 11, 12, 13, 14, 15, 16, 18, 19, 21, 24, 26,
27, 28, 29, 33, 34, 37, 54, 62, 63, 71, 78, 79,
80, 81, 83, 84; **Neil Setchfield:** pages 6, 22,
70, 90; **Jonathan Smith:** pages 7, 10, 20, 25,
47, 51, 52 (right), 65.

**Front Cover:** The Castle District abounds with
gorgeous architecture.
**Title Page:** A view of the Parliament building
across the Danube.

# CONTENTS

## MAKE THE MOST OF YOUR GUIDE

Reading these two pages will help you to get the most out of your guide and save you time when using it. Sites discussed in the text are cross-referenced with the cover maps – for example, the reference 'Map B–C3' refers to the Central Budapest Map (Map B), column C, row 3. Use the Map Plan below to quickly locate the map you need.

### MAP PLAN

Outside Back Cover                    Outside Front Cover

Inside Front Cover                    Inside Back Cover

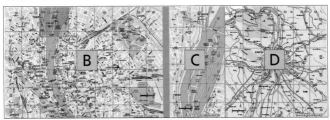

THE BIGGER PICTURE

**Key to Map Plan**

A – Budapest Public Transport Map
B – Central Budapest
C – Margaret Island
D – Around Budapest
E – Lake Balaton
F – Excursions

# USING THIS BOOK

## Key to Symbols

⊠ – address

☎ – telephone

🖰 – fax

🖳 – website

🖰 – e-mail address

🕐 – opening times

💰 – entry fee

🍽 – restaurants nearby

🚌 – tours

**M** – nearest Metro station

## Map Legend

| | | |
|---|---|---|
| motorway | main road | Kossuth L. u. |
| national road | other road | Petőfi Sándor u. |
| main road | mall | VÁC U. |
| minor road | HÉV line | HÉV |
| railway | built-up area | |
| ferry route | building of interest | National Archives |
| route number `9` `3215` | | |
| river Bér-p. | shopping centre | Ⓢ Westend Centre |
| dam | museum | ▦ |
| city **BUDAPEST** | university | ■ |
| major town ◉ Esztergom | library | 🖾 |
| town ○ Gödöllő | post office | ⊠ |
| large village ◎ Dunakeszi | tourist information | ⓘ |
| village ○ Csomád | | |
| airport ✈ ✈ | place of interest | ★ Szondy |
| cave ☋ | hotel | Ⓗ RADISSON SAS BEKE |
| castle ♜ | place of worship | △ |
| border post ✦ | | |
| viewpoint ⱡ | police station | ● |
| | bus terminus | 🚍 |
| park & garden Vidám Park | hospital | ⊕ |

## Keep us Current

Travel information is apt to change, which is why we regularly update our guides. We'd be most grateful to receive feedback from you if you've noted something we should include in our updates. If you have any new information, please share it with us by writing to the Publishing Manager, Globetrotter, at the office nearest to you (addresses on the imprint page of this guide). The most significant contribution to each new edition will be rewarded with a free copy of the updated guide.

## BUDAPEST
### The Land

Hungary may well be among Europe's smaller nations, yet it packs tremendous variety into its 93,030 km² (35,919 sq miles). The country is located within the **Carpathian Basin** in central Europe, bordered by Austria, Slovakia, Croatia, Serbia and Montenegro, Ukraine, Romania and Slovenia. It is split down the middle by the Danube River, which enters in the northwest, divides the capital Budapest, and exits in the south near Mohács.

**Budapest** is home to two million people. It straddles the Danube, with its two constituent parts, Buda and Pest, on opposite banks. Some 40km (25 miles) upstream, where the big river takes a 90-degree turn south between hills, is the scenic area called the **Danube Bend**, centred on the towns of Esztergom, Visegrád and Vác.

### Climate

Hungary sits at the confluence of Europe's key climatic zones, which causes weather patterns to vary from region to region. In the eastern half of the country the climate is broadly **continental**, but in the west and south it is influenced by the **Atlantic** and the **Mediterranean** respectively.

In Budapest, spring's early arrival is followed by a showery May and June and warm summer that can become quite humid in the capital. The July temperature in Budapest averages 21°C (70°F); in January it plummets to –1°C (30°F).

---

**Facts and Figures**
- Hungary is 93,030km² (35,919 sq miles) in area – it comprises one per cent of the total area of Europe.
- From west to east, Hungary is 528km (328 miles); from north to south 320km (198 miles). Its border measures 2242km (1393 miles).
- Hungary's highest point is Kékes, in the Mátra Hills, at 1014m (3326ft).
- Lake Balaton is Hungary's largest lake and Europe's largest freshwater lake outside Scandinavia. Its area is 598km² (230 sq miles).
- Hungary's population just exceeds 10 million, of whom 63 per cent live in cities and towns. Budapest's population is two million.

## History in Brief

In the first few years of Christianity, the **Romans** under Emperor Augustus occupied the area of Hungary south of the Danube and established the province of **Pannonia**. They established several **garrison towns**, including Aquincum – on the site of Óbuda suburb in present-day Budapest – which was to become the capital of Lower Pannonia.

Roman withdrawal from Pannonia began in the 4th century – creating a power vacuum that was seized by the **Huns** under **Attila**. The Huns took Aquincum in 430AD, but capitulated after Attila's death. The **Avars** added the thinly populated territory to the Avar Empire in the 6th century and a period of relative calm ensued before they, too, were conquered.

### Marauding Magyars

Seven tribes – up to 500,000 people in all and led by **Prince Árpád**, now recognized as the first great Hungarian leader – swept westwards in 896 and crossed the Carpathians to seize control of the Basin, thus establishing one of the key dates in Hungarian history. They were known collectively as the **Magyars**.

Defeated by **Henry of Saxony** in 933, and again by **King Otto I** in 955, there were two options for the Magyars – to form themselves into a civilized state or to disappear off the map altogether. **Grand Prince Géza**, great-grandson of Árpád and leader of the Magyars after 972, took the former route – and embraced Christianity.

> **The Danube**
> The Danube, which bisects Budapest, is Europe's second longest river after the Volga, and the principal river of Central Europe. It flows into Hungary at the northwestern tip and leaves it in the south, near Mohács – some 417km (259 miles) of its total 2850km (1770 miles) are in Hungary. The Tisza is Hungary's other main river, with 596km (370 miles) in Hungary; the Dráva, a tributary of the Danube, is Hungary's third longest river.

**Opposite:** *A view over Budapest, the capital city of Hungary, towards the Buda Hills.*
**Below**: *The Danube, Europe's second longest river, flows through Budapest.*

**Opposite:** *Imre Nagy's statue recalls the man at the centre of the 1956 Uprising.*
**Below:** *King Stephen's crown, one of Hungary's treasures.*

## Kingdom of Hungary

Catholic missionaries were invited to Hungary and Géza and his son Vajk, who later adopted the Christian name István (Stephen), were baptized. On Christmas Day in 1000, Stephen was crowned Hungary's first king; papal approval had been sought from Rome and Pope Sylvester II provided the crown at Stephen's request. Under King Stephen I the emergent Christian state began to strengthen its ties with the West. The death of **Andrew III** without an heir in 1301 ended the 400-year rule of the House of Árpád; for the bulk of the next two centuries Hungary was ruled by a succession of foreign kings.

## Turks and Habsburgs

The Hungarians suffered badly at the hands of **Sultan Suleiman I** (Suleiman the Magnificent) in 1526. **Turkish occupation** of Buda followed in 1541 and Hungary split into three parts for the next century and a half. What was left of the Kingdom of Hungary in the north and west was occupied by the **Habsburgs**. In the end Hungary was no more than a province of the Habsburg empire.

The revolution of 1848–49 that ended in the War of Independence began with a **rebellion** in March 1848. Led by the Hungarian poet **Sándor Petőfi**, it called for establishing a responsible government, freedom of the press and the abolition of serfdom.

## Independence

In 1867, a compromise with the Habsburgs, aimed at stemming demand for home rule, created the

Austro-Hungarian Empire, in which Hungary had self-government while sharing defence and foreign ministries with the Austrians. In 1873, the three cities of Buda, Pest and Óbuda were merged to form the capital, Budapest.

## World Wars I and II

As part of the Austro-Hungarian federation, Hungarians were forced to fight on the German Empire's side in World War I. They entered the war in July 1914, exactly one month after the murder of the Habsburg Archduke Franz Ferdinand in Sarajevo. Hundreds of thousands of Hungarians perished on the Russian and Italian fronts.

After the outbreak of World War II in 1939, Hungary called on Nazi support to secure the return of northern Transylvania by Romania in July 1940 and a portion of Croatia the following year – but at an enormous price.

By June 1941, Hungary was embroiled in a war that was to prove as costly to the country in human terms as the 1914–18 conflict. Hungarian soldiers joined the Axis forces in the invasion of the USSR in 1941, and during the course of World War II, Hungary lost some 140,000 soldiers. By April 1945, only a quarter of Budapest's buildings were left intact and every Danube bridge had been destroyed.

## Under the Communists

The Communists, led by Mátyás Rákosi, seized power in 1947. The Communists and Social Democrats merged to become the Hungarian Socialist Workers' Party. After Stalin's death in 1953, Moscow's more moderate leadership replaced prime minister Rákosi with the mod-

### Imre Nagy
Imre Nagy, Hungarian prime minister from 1953–55, was the key figure at the centre of the 1956 Uprising. Frustrated in his reform efforts, he was expelled from the Communist Party in 1955 but re-admitted a year later. During 1956, student calls in Budapest and Szeged to have him re-instated as prime minister sparked the uprising. For a few days Nagy led a hastily formed government of neutrality before the Soviet tanks rolled in. He was among 2000 people executed in the aftermath of the revolt and died on 16 June 1958 after a secret trial.

**Above:** *Hungary's flag was formally adopted in 1848.*

erate Communist Imre Nagy (*see* panel, page 9). Unfortunately, Nagy's reform plans were blocked by the old guard and he was kicked out of the party, but the seeds of anti-regime protest had been sown, first in literature and then in debates. Increasing dissatisfaction led to the Hungarian Uprising of 1956.

### The 1956 Uprising

What started as a student demonstration on 23 October 1956 in support of reforms in Poland quickly became one of support for Nagy, and escalated into the major uprising that cost many lives and caused some 200,000 Hungarians to flee to the West. Within days, Nagy had installed an interim coalition government; by 1 November he had issued a declaration of neutrality and withdrawal from the Warsaw Pact. This action brought swift reprisals. Soviet reinforcements crossed the Hungarian border on 1 November and three days later tanks lumbered into Budapest.

As the street fighting raged, a new government was installed under the leadership of former interior minister János Kádár (*see* panel, page 11). Hungary now trod a more liberalized path within the communist framework.

### The Curtain Comes Down

In October 1989, exactly 33 years after the uprising, the **Republic of Hungary** was proclaimed, and in October 1990 the communists were crushed by a centre-right coalition led by **József Antall** in the first multiparty elections.

Within five years of the Iron Curtain's collapse, the reformed communists came into power in a coalition with the Free Democrats.

In 2000 Hungary applied to join the European Union, seeing its future in a united Europe. It was formally admitted on 1 May 2004, along with nine other nations.

## Government and Economy

When the **Iron Curtain** fell, Hungary's economy was prepared for the privatization of its industry. But growth in the early years proved difficult, and Hungarians struggled to come to terms with the fact that they had been better off under the communist regime; they found the reality of a **market economy** unbelievably harsh. Exacerbating the problem were economic difficulties among Hungary's former Eastern Bloc trading partners and the **general recession** of the time. **Unemployment** soared to Western proportions – from 0.5 per cent to 12.5 per cent between 1989 and 1993.

**Privatization** continued through the 1990s towards the 100 per cent level demanded by the government, at first involving foreign investors and then also embracing local investment. Over the decade, Hungary received the lion's share of foreign funding that was ploughed into countries of the now defunct **East European Comecon** trading group.

**Liberal Leader**
When János Kádár – who had served in Imre Nagy's government – joined the Communists and was made prime minister in September 1956, with Soviet tanks still on Budapest's streets, he was the most reviled man in Hungary. But though Kádár served as prime minister from 1956–58 and 1961–65, his liberal policies improved the standard of living among Hungary's people. Under Kádár, Hungary embraced 'market socialism' and became known as 'the most cheerful barracks in the socialist camp'. Unable to deal with soaring inflation and a growing national debt, he was dismissed in 1988 and died the next year, aged 77.

**Below:** *Hungarian Parliament sits in session.*

### Hungarian Artists
- Bertalan Székely (1835–1910)
- Gyula Benczúr (1844–1920)
- Mihály Munkácsy (1844–1900)
- Kosztka Tivadar Csontváry (1853–1919)
- József Rippl-Rónai (1861–1927)

### Hungarian Musicians
- Ferenc Erkel (1810–93)
- Franz (Ferenc) Liszt (1811–86)
- Béla Bartók (1881–1945)
- Zoltán Kodály (1882–1967)

**Opposite:** *A bust of the 19th-century Romantic novelist Mór Jokai.*
**Below:** *Traditional costume is worn in Hungary's villages.*

Hungary's industrial revival in the latter 1990s saw the production of vehicles, pharmaceuticals and electronic goods become key industries. **Communications** have taken a turn for the better, with improved roads and a modernized telephone system.

The spur for Hungary's economic improvement was its drive for membership of the **EU**, with whose members Hungary was conducting more than 60 per cent of its foreign trade. Hungary, Poland and the Czech Republic were among 10 nations admitted to the EU on 1 May 2004 – the biggest single expansion of the EU that brought membership up to a total of 25 countries. Meanwhile, the political spectrum has narrowed after the initial post-communism euphoria that saw the rise to varying degrees of prominence of parties such as the Hungarian Democratic Forum, Christian Democrats, Smallholders and Young Democrats' Federation.

With the extremes of right or left having been endured for most of the past 60 years, Hungary's immediate political future now appears to lie in a more **centrist** government, whether a single party or power-sharing coalition.

## The People

Hungary's **population** has been in decline for a quarter of a century and now numbers around 10.1 million. This includes an estimated 400,000 Romanies (gypsies) and 200,000 Germans – plus Croats, Romanians, Slovaks and Serbs.

From the Magyar conquest onwards, Hungary has welcomed foreign settlers and today they live mainly in the border regions. The ethnic minorities have rights enshrined under Hungarian law. The **Hungarian constitution** guarantees freedom and equality – and the free use of language – to the country's 22 ethnic minorities and 82 Romany organizations.

Meanwhile, approximately five million Magyars live outside Hungary's borders, with the Transylvania region of Romania home to more than two million of them. Magyars also live in Slovakia, Serbia, Montenegro, Croatia and Ukraine.

**Life expectancy** among Hungarian men is low by European standards at 68 years; 15 years ago it was just 65, with only 54 per cent reaching that age. Women can expect to live eight years longer – and are noticeably in the majority in Hungary.

Transdanubia and Budapest were first to feel the **modernizing** influences of Western Europe – in contrast to the eastern part of the country, where traditions are deeply rooted and the old Hungarian character – shaped by pride, vanity and commitment to freedom – is still very much in evidence.

## Language

**Hungarian** is among Europe's oldest languages, spoken by 15 million people. It's also one of the most difficult to learn. **Ethnic** groups within Hungary's borders do not have **dialects** to worry about and communication doesn't usually present a problem.

For visitors who don't speak Hungarian, German is the best alternative; English is understood reasonably well in Budapest, but less so outside the capital. Try a little basic Hungarian: your efforts will be most appreciated.

---

<u>Literature</u>
The first Hungarian to have had international literary impact was the poet **Sándor Petőfi** (1823–49). His friend **János Arany** (1817–82) was a prominent Romantic poet. **Endre Ady** (1877–1919) is credited with being the founder of modern Hungarian poetry; other poets include **Attila József** (1905–37) and **Gyula Illyés** (1902–83) Important modern authors include **György Konrád** (b 1933), **Péter Nádas** (b 1942), **György Petri** (b 1943) and **Péter Esterházy** (b 1950). Konrád's contribution has been of particular value in providing a literary record of Hungarian history.

⊕ *See* Map B–B4   ★★★

**House of Wines**
The best way to sample Hungarian viticulture is to dive into the cellars at the House of Wines in the Castle District, where you can enjoy up to 80 wines from the country's 20 wine regions. As you 'tour' the country, taste buds at the ready and glass in hand, you can read about wine production in each of the regions.

## CASTLE DISTRICT

Streets of the **Várnegyed** (Castle District) spread northwest of **Szentháromság tér**, in the middle of which stands the **Holy Trinity Column**. Built in 1710–13 by grateful citizens to mark the end of a plague, it stands before the **Matthias Church**, on the highest point of Castle Hill. On the square you will also find the **House of Hungarian Wines**, occupying the cellars of the one-time Finance Ministry building.

Fisherman's Bastion, the Matthias Church and King Stephen's statue are reflected in the copper-coloured glass windows of Béla Pintér's **Budapest Hilton Hotel**, built in 1976 and incorporating the remains of a medieval Dominican church and 17th-century Jesuit college. The hotel fronts Hess Andras tér, with its statue of **Pope Innocent XI**. At No. 3 is one of the district's oldest houses, from the late 14th century, with a small red hedgehog relief above the doorway.

The **Hungarian Museum of Commerce and Catering** takes a peep into past times of Budapest's hospitality industry, with its century-old exhibits. The **Music History Museum**, in the Baroque **Erdödy Palace**, has instruments, manuscripts, medals and paintings with a musical theme. An exhibition is devoted to the illustrious musical career of the great Hungarian composer **Béla Bartók**, who had a workshop here.

**Below and opposite:** *Fascinating old buildings line the streets of Budapest's Castle District.*

The **Medieval Jewish Prayer House** at No. 26 in the same street has artefacts relating to Jewish life in Buda; in addition, more comprehensive documentation of Budapest's Jewish community can be found in the **Jewish Museum**.

The **Vienna Gate** is a reconstruction of an earlier entrance through the city walls; it dates from 1936. Next to the gate is the massive stone-fronted **National Archives** building with its diamond-patterned tiled roof complementing that of the Matthias Church.

Past the National Archives is the **Mary Magdalene Tower** on Kapisztrán tér, all that is left of a large 13th-century church that was destroyed in World War II. A **carillon** of two dozen small bells on the exterior of the tower plays Hungarian folk tunes and other medleys at various times of day.

Across the square from the tower is the **Military History Museum**. It is housed in a former barracks stretching alongside the promenade of Tóth Árpád sétány. The museum contains a library, archives and map room, and frequently mounts exhibitions.

At the end of the promenade is the **grave of Abdurrahman**, the last Turkish ruler of Budapest, who was killed in 1686. The inscription calls him a 'valiant foe'.

Back on the square is the **statue** of **Friar John Kapisztrán** with a vanquished Turk – he inspired the Hungarians to victory over the Turks in the siege of Belgrade in 1456.

**House of Hungarian Wines**
✉ Szentháromság tér 6, across from the Matthias Church,
☎ 212 1031
🕐 daily 12:00–20:00

**Hungarian Museum of Commerce and Catering**
✉ Fortuna utca 4
☎ 375 6249
🕐 Wed–Fri 10:00–17:00, Sat–Sun 10:00–18:00

**Music History Museum**
✉ Erdödy Palace, Táncsics Mihály utca 7
☎ 214 6770
🕐 Tue–Sun 10:00–18:00

**Military History Museum**
✉ Tóth Árpád sétány 40
☎ 356 9522
🕐 Tue–Sat 10:00–17:00, Sun 10:00–18:00

⊙ *See* Map B–B4     ★★★

## MATTHIAS CHURCH

The church looks older than it is – mostly a neo-Gothic design of the late 19th century by architect **Frigyes Schulek**. It was named after the 15th-century Renaissance king and incorporates parts of a 13th-century church that once occupied the site.

On your left through the solid wooden doors is the **coat of arms** of King Matthias, who married Beatrice of Aragon here; at its centre the raven and ring representing the family name Corvinus.

The church's richly painted **interior** has very few equals – pillars, walls, arches and vaulting of dark red and gold motifs beneath a canopy of blue and gold. A number

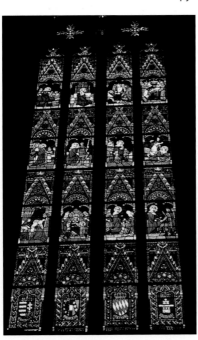

of large **frescoes** occupy the spaces between the abstract geometrics on the walls, mostly the work of **Károly Lotz** and **Bertalan Székely**, two eminent Romantic painters of the day.

The **crypt** (which has a small admission charge) contains ecclesiastical exhibits; from here stairs lead up to the highly decorated **St Stephen's Chapel**, at its entrance a bust of Queen Elizabeth (1837–98), known as 'Sissy', by **György Zala**.

It was in St Matthias Church, at the coronation of Emperor Franz

See Map B–B4 ★★★

Josef I and Elizabeth as king and queen of Hungary in 1867, that Franz Liszt's **Coronation Mass** was first performed, having been composed specifically for the occasion.

Up a narrow staircase is the **Royal Oratory**, where replicas of Hungary's crown jewels – King Stephen's crown, orb and sceptre – are displayed and the making of the crown explained in detail. Robes and chalices line an upper gallery.

## FISHERMAN'S BASTION

Behind the church, the fairytale structure with its five turrets flanking a main tower is the Fisherman's Bastion, built in 1890–1905 by **Schulek** as a promenade from which to admire his ecclesiastical work on one side and the fine view along the Danube on the other. Upstream are the Buda Hills and green Margaret Island, across the river the best view to be had of the Parliament building, and to your right, on the opposite bank beyond the Chain Bridge, a clutch of riverside five-star hotels – the Sofitel Atrium, Inter-Continental and Marriott.

Fishermen from the Víziváros district below the hill were said to have defended this area during the Middle Ages; it was also the site of a fish market. By the bastion is a splendid equestrian statue of King Stephen wearing both crown and halo – it is widely held to be the finest of all the capital's statues.

**Above:** *The distinctive towers of the Fisherman's Bastion.*
**Opposite:** *The Matthias Church has fine stained-glass windows.*

---

**Matthias Church**
✉ Szentháromsag tér
☎ 355 5657
🖥 www.matyas-tempom.hu
🕘 Mon–Sat 09:00–17:00, Sun 13:00–17:00
💰 Fts 600 (adults), Fts 300 (students, seniors), children under 6 free; audioguide Fts 300
Ⓜ Moszkva tér, then Várbusz (Castle Hill bus)

**Fisherman's Bastion**
✉ Szentháromsag tér
💰 free
Ⓜ Moszkva tér, then Várbusz (Castle Hill bus)

17

⊛ *See* Map B–B5      ★★★

## ROYAL PALACE

The Royal Palace has its origins in medieval times. The first castle on the site was built by **Béla IV** around 1255 following the Mongol invasion; the Renaissance palace of **Matthias Corvinus** (1458–90) was one of the best until its destruction during the siege that ended the Turkish occupation in 1686.

The **Habsburgs** redeveloped the site, expanding their version of the palace through the 19th century, though it was never inhabited by them. The Royal Palace became **Admiral Horthy's** headquarters until he was forced out by the Nazis in 1944; in the subsequent Red Army siege of Buda, the **Nazis** made their last stand in the palace, which was left in ruins.

The Royal Palace you see today, with its added dome, mostly dates from the 1950s and has a **museum and art gallery complex**. Within are the Hungarian National Gallery, the Budapest History Museum (Castle Museum), and also the National Széchenyi Library.

The **Magyar Nemzeti Galéria (Hungarian National Gallery**, wings A, B, C and D) contains Hungarian pieces dating from the Middle Ages right up to the present time – it is quite an overwhelming collection incorporating a medieval and Renaissance lapidarium, some Gothic altarpieces, sculptures and panel paintings, along with canvases of the leading Hungarian artists.

---

**The *Turul***
The menacing bronze bird of prey, its talons grasping a sword, sitting above a gateway to the Royal Palace is the *turul*. The mythological bird is said to have made the grandmother of Prince Árpád pregnant, thus siring the early generations of Hungarian kings and earning its place in Hungarian history. It was adopted by the Hungarians as a **unifying symbol** against the Austrians and in recent years has become associated with far-right political elements.

**Below:** *The* turul *bird by the Royal Palace gateway.*

*See* Map B–B5    ★★★

Some of the big names whose work is exhibited include **Mihály Munkácsy**, **László Paál**, **Gyula Benczúr**, the Impressionist **Pál Merse Szinyei**, the noted portrait painter **József Rippl-Rónai** (*see* panel, page 38), and the renowned landscape artist **Tivadar Csontváry** (*see* panel, page 39), whose work posthumously drew praise from Picasso.

At the far end of Lion Courtyard (the work of János Fadrusz in 1904) is the **Budapesti Történeti Múzeum (Budapest History Museum**, *see* page 36). The **Országos Széchenyi Könyvtár (National Széchenyi Library**, *see* page 38) also has its entrance in Lion Courtyard.

Recently moved from the Royal Palace is the **Kortárs Müvestzí Múzeum (Museum of Contemporary Art**, *see* page 38), known as the Ludwig Museum after its founder, German industrialist Peter Ludwig. The museum is now at the contemporary **Palace of Arts** by the Lágymányosi Bridge.

**Above:** *The Royal Palace houses a museum and art gallery complex.*

---

**Hungarian National Gallery**
✉ Buda Castle, Royal Palace, Wings A, B, C and D
☎ (20) 4397 325/331
📠 212 7356
🖥 www.mng.hu
🕐 Tue–Sun 10:00–18:00; dome is open Tue–Sun 10:00–17:00
💰 free; dome Fts 300
Ⓜ Moszkva tér, then Várbusz (Castle Hill bus)

🌐 *See* Map B–D3 ★★★

## PARLIAMENT BUILDING

The riverside Parliament building, styled by **Imre Steindl** on London's Palace of Westminster, was completed in 1902, having been 17 years in the making. This grand neo-Gothic edifice, with its 691 rooms and 18 courtyards, stretches 268m (293yd) along the Danube; its cupola is 96m (315ft) high, marking the date of the Magyars' conquest of Hungary in 896. Sadly, the building was faced with porous limestone, necessitating ongoing renovation work. There are daily tours in English at 10:00, 12:00, 14:00 and 18:00; it now houses the Hungarian crown jewels.

The two large buildings facing Parliament across Kossuth tér are the **Ministry of Agriculture** on the right and **Ethnography Museum** (*see* page 37) on the left.

Following the east bank of the Danube beyond the Parliament building brings you to **Margit híd** (Margaret Bridge), providing access to **Margaret Island** (*see* page 25). The road off the bridge brings you shortly to Budapest's Western station by Nyugati tér.

---

**The Crown Jewels**
Hungary's most treasured possessions are the **crown**, surmounted by its bent cross, **orb** and **sceptre** known collectively as the **Coronation Regalia**. The crown is said to be that used at the coronation of King Stephen in 1000, but experts doubt this; in any case, it is early medieval and the undisputed symbol of the Hungarian state. Last used by the Habsburg king Charles VI in 1916 and carried off to Germany by fascists in 1945, the crown was at last returned to Hungary from storage at Fort Knox (USA) in 1978. The jewels were moved from the Hungarian National Museum in 2000 and are now housed in the Parliament building.

☆ *See Map B–E4*  ★★★

## THE HUNGARIAN STATE OPERA HOUSE

The straight and grand boulevard of **Andrássy út** (at one time Stalin Avenue) heads northeast from Deák tér, and five minutes' walk past the **Post Office Museum** on your right brings you before the neo-Renaissance **Magyar Állami Operaház (Hungarian State Opera House)** built in 1884. It looks good on the outside – and it's even better within, all gilded and marble-clad with fine frecoes, the creation of Miklós Ybl, and containing the output of leading 19th-century Hungarian painters. It seats around 1300 concert-goers. **Statues** of composers **Ferenc Erkel**, the writer of Hungary's national anthem, and **Franz Liszt** flank the main entrance. If you can't make a performance, take an afternoon tour, for which tickets can be bought at an office situated to the right of the building.

Dating from the same period, the former **Hungarian Dance Academy** located directly opposite is the creation of leading Art Nouveau builder **Ödön Lechner** and strikes a nice balance across Andrássy út – it is to become a hotel.

Situated to the rear of the Academy, the **Új Színház (New Theatre)** at Paulay Ede utca 35 is a steely grey Art Deco building adorned with monkeys above the doorway and gold and blue decoration aloft.

**Star Composer**
**Franz (Ferenc) Liszt** (1811–86) is remembered as Hungary's leading Romantic composer; also as pianist and founder of the **Academy of Music** in the Budapest house in which he lived from 1881 until his death (Vörösmarty utca 35, now the **Liszt Museum**). Liszt did not settle in Budapest until 1875, after spells in Paris, Weimar and Rome. His output was prodigious. In 1856, his *Esztergom Mass* was chosen to be performed for the consecration of the new **Esztergom Basilica**. In 1867, he composed the *Coronation Mass* for the crowning of Emperor **Franz Joseph I** as king of Hungary.

**Opposite:** *Stately Parliament building.*
**Below:** *Budapest's State Opera House.*

🌀 *See* Map B–D4   ★★★

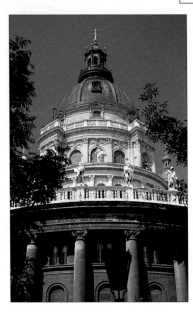

**Above:** *The dome of St Stephen's Basilica.*

## ST STEPHEN'S BASILICA

From Deák tér, the dome of St Stephen's Basilica, Budapest's cathedral, appears above the Erzsébet Téri cultural park. The lengthy restoration that has required much of the building to be scaffolded is now complete. Restoration has also been taking place on the interior, with its abundance of marble, gilding and frescoes.

Work on the Basilica started under **József Hild** in 1851, but was not completed for another 54 years – in no small way because the dome collapsed during a storm in January 1868. With fresh plans drawn up by **Miklós Ybl**, designer of the Hungarian State Opera House, the building was begun again almost from scratch and, following Ybl's death in 1891, completed by **József Kauser** in 1905.

In a gold casket before **Our Lady's Altar** is the mummified **right hand of St Stephen**, Hungary's most venerated possession. It found its way to Budapest in 1771, having been kept in Transylvania, Ragusa (the present Dubrovnik) and Vienna; spirited away to the West in 1944 during World War II, it was returned after the war. The **Panorama Tower** gives an excellent overview of Pest; the **Treasury** contains some prized artefacts.

**St Stephen's Basilica**
✉ Szent István tér 33
☎ 317 2859
📠 338 2151
📧 cathedral@basilica.hu
💻 www.basilica.hu
🕐 09:00–17:30; services daily 07:00–09:00, 17:30–20:00
💰 free; small charge for tower and treasury
Ⓜ Bajcsy-Zsilinszky út, Arany János utca

☆ *See* Map B–E5

★★★

## HUNGARIAN NATIONAL MUSEUM

A block north of the **Kecskemét Gate** on Múzeum körút is the neo-Classical **Magyar Nemzeti Múzeum (Hungarian National Museum)**, the largest in Hungary, within its leafy grounds. Designed by **Mihály Polláck**, it opened in 1847 and traces Hungarian history from the arrival of the Magyars to 1990. The crown jewels formerly housed here are now on show in the Parliament building (*see* page 20). A significant date in the museum's long history is 15 March 1848, when eminent poet Sándor Petőfi delivered the words of the patriotic **National Song** from its steps – firing the revolution against the Habsburgs that led to the War of Independence. The National Museum is a focal point of celebrations marking the national holiday on 15 March.

**Poet and Patriot**
**Sándor Petőfi**, who lived a short life between 1823 and 1849, was Hungary's greatest poet – compared with Robert Burns and studied by Hungarian children, yet relatively unknown outside his home country. His statue in Petőfi tér, at the Pest end of Elizabeth Bridge, is by Miklós Izso and Adolf Huszar. Erected in 1882, it shows Petőfi reciting his patriotic anthem '*Talpre, Magyar*' ('Rise up, Hungarians') that sparked the **1848 War of Independence** against the Habsburgs. The patriotic young poet died at the age of 26 in battle.

**Hungarian National Museum**
✉ Muzeum körút 14–16
☎ 338 2122
🖷 317 7806
⌨ nemzetimuzeum.budapest@museum.hu
🖳 www.museum.hu/budapest/nemzeti muzeum
🕘 Tue–Sun 10:00–18:00
🍽 café (inexpensive)
💰 Fts 800 (students Fts 400)
Ⓜ Kálvin tér

**Left:** *The imposing façade of the Hungarian National Museum.*

⊙ See Map B–G2    ★★

## HEROES' SQUARE

The vast expanse of **Hősök tere (Heroes' Square)**, with its neo-Classical museum and exhibition buildings flanking the **Millenary Monument** and **colonnade**, leaves a lasting impression.

**Above:** *Chieftains of the seven Magyar tribes stand proudly at the foot of the Millenary Monument and Colonnade on Heroes' Square.*

---

**The Magyars**

The seven original Magyar tribes originated in Asia rather than Europe, having evolved as an ethnic group between 1000BC and 500BC on the south-western slopes of the Ural Mountains. The Magyars' first migration from their Magna Hungaria homeland to the Black Sea took place between 700AD and 750AD; around 400,000 strong, they arrived in the Carpathian Basin in 896. Both syllables of the name Magyar – *mogy* and *eri* – mean 'man'; the name Magyar was later adopted by the country and its people.

---

The square was created in 1896 to commemorate the 1000th anniversary of the Magyars' arrival in the Carpathian Basin. Atop the 36m (118ft) column is the **Archangel Gabriel**, who is said to have appeared in a dream to Stephen and offered him the Hungarian crown; at the base of the column are chieftains of the **seven original Magyar tribes**. The colonnade of two semicircles carries **statues** of leading Hungarian rulers, from King Stephen down the centuries. In front is the **Tomb of the Unknown Soldier**.

The larger of the two imposing neo-Classical buildings is the **Szépmüvészeti Múzeum (Museum of Fine Arts**, *see* page 38). Across the square is the **Műcsarnok**, Hungary's biggest exhibition hall, with large rooms for staging short-term exhibitions. The six-lane cobbled avenue to the right facing the Palace of Arts, Dózsa György út, was Hungary's version of Red Square, where communist leaders carried out military reviews under the watchful eye of **Lenin** – the statue is now in the Statue Park (*see* page 40).

☆ *See* Map C     ★★

## MARGARET ISLAND

North from Margaret Bridge is Margaret Island and the pointed monument resembling a giant cracked-open seed pod is the **Centennial Monument**, erected in 1973 to commemorate the centenary of the joining of Buda, Pest and Óbuda into the present-day capital city. It's one of the city's odder monuments; as well as the three shields, the inside contains cogwheels, helmets, knives and other miscellany.

The **National Swimming Pool** here was built in the 1930s by **Alfréd Hajós** (1878–1955), Hungarian winner of the 100m and 1200m swimming events at the first Olympiad in Athens in 1896. Also on the island, the **Palatinus Strand** complex is another swimmers' idyll, with outdoor thermal pools, water slides and terraces for sunbathing.

Two walls and a crumbling tower are all that remain of a 13th-century **Franciscan Church**. Diagonally across the park is another ruin – that of the former **Dominican Church and Convent**. A little way further on is an octagonal **Water Tower** (1911), with a café at its base flanking an open-air theatre; hereabouts, busts of several Hungarian worthies are dotted among the trees.

Nearby is the tiny **St Michael's Premonstratensian Church** (*see* page 35). At the north end of the island are the two large **spa hotels** of the Danubius Group – the Grand and the Thermal.

**Palatinus Strand**
✉ Margitsziget
(Margaret Island)
☎ 340 4505
🕐 May, Mon–Fri
10:00–18:00, Sat–Sun
09:00–19:00; Jun–Aug
Mon–Sun 09:00–19:00,
last entry 18:00
🚌 bus 26 from
Nyugati pu.
♿ admission to all
pools Fts 1400 adults,
Fts 1200 children and
teenagers, Fts 600 after
17:00 Mon–Fri

**Below:** *The Water Tower, nearly a century old, peeps out above the trees on leafy Margaret Island.*

**Aquincum Museum**
✉ Szentendrei út 139
☎ 250 1650
📱 430 1083
🖂 aquincum.budapest
@museum.hu
💻 www.aquincum.hu
🕐 15–30 Apr and
1–31 Oct 10:00–17:00;
May–Sep 10:00–18:00
M Aquincum (HÉV)

**Opposite:** *Meet the elegant umbrella ladies of Óbuda, an inspired creation by Imre Varga.*
**Below:** *The museum and wall foundations of the Roman town of Aquincum.*

✪ *See* Map D–C3   ★★

## AQUINCUM

A 20-minute ride on the HÉV suburban train from Batthyány tér station brings you to Aquincum – and what is left of the **Roman town** that was the provincial **capital of Lower Pannonia**, close to the Roman Empire's Danube frontier. You can identify the streets, forum, temples, public baths (one containing a mosaic of wrestlers), market hall, shops and houses of the Roman civilian town from the wall foundations. The **military base** with its 6000 soldiers was sited in Óbuda (Old Buda), around present-day Flórián tér, where only a few scattered remains are now visible.

Aquincum prospered in the 2nd and 3rd centuries. Sacked on several occasions in the 3rd and 4th centuries, it eventually fell to the Huns early in the 5th century.

The **museum**, in neo-Classical style, was built in 1894 and contains a variety of artefacts from the site, including a reconstructed water organ from the period. Across Szentendrei út is the **amphitheatre**, the Romans' cultural and leisure centre.

This was Aquincum's venue for concerts, plays and sporting contests, attended by up to 4000 enthusiastic citizens at a time – it was also the scene of gladiator contests and animal fights. Next to the amphitheatre were the **gladiators' barracks**.

See Map C–A1 ★★

## ÓBUDA

The heart of Óbuda – which all but lost its identity in 1873 when it was merged with the new Budapest – is a short walk from Árpád híd station on the HÉV suburban railway. Its centre is **Flórián tér**; here are the yellow Baroque **Óbuda Parish Church** and the former **Óbuda Synagogue**, now TV studios. Nearby, at Meggyfa utca 19–21, is **Hercules Villa**, named after the 3rd-century floor mosaic of a former Roman villa.

North of Árpád híd is picturesque **Fő tér**, with its restored collection of Baroque houses and restaurants in a quaint village-like atmosphere. The former Zichy mansion on Szentlékek tér contains the **Vasarely Museum** (*see* page 39) and the **Kassák Museum**, with work from the early 20th century. The **Zsigmond Kun Collection** of folk art occupies an 18th-century town-house at Fő tér 4. Four unhappy ladies with bright shiny umbrellas wait beneath a lam-post on Laktanya utca – the creation of **Imre Varga**, whose work is displayed fur-ther down the street in a gallery at No. 7.

On Pacsirtamező utca are the remains of the Roman military **amphitheatre**; even larger than the Colisseum in Rome, it could hold 15,000 spectators.

---

### Gül Baba's Tomb

A steep cobbled street rising from near the Buda end of Margit híd (Margaret Bridge) leads to the tomb of Gül Baba, a 16th-century Muslim whose name means 'Father of the Roses'. He took part in the Turks' capture of Buda in 1541, founded the Bektashi order in Buda, and planted the roses on **Rószadomb (Rose Hill)** to the southwest. His coffin is located in the small octagonal building reached up a flight of steps; the site has been restored by the Turkish government.

| 🌀 *See* Map B–C6 | ★ |

**Above:** *Gellért Hill offers grand views of the capital.*

---

**Grand Old Lady**
The **Gellért**, which opened in 1918, is Budapest's grand old hotel – a world-famous Art Nouveau property that has hosted generations of celebrities down the years. The Gellért's main **thermal bath** is one of the wonders of Budapest, with its high columns, majolica tiles and lion water-spouts. It is entered on the right side of the hotel, on Kelenhegyi út. You will also find outdoor swimming and thermal pools here.
✉ Szent Gellért tér 1
☎ 889 5500
📠 889 5505
🕀 gellert.reservation@
danubiusgroup.com
🖥 www.danubius
hotels.com/gellert

## GELLÉRT HILL

On this quiet tree-shrouded hill, the noise of the city rushes up to meet you. Steps and pathways lead upwards to the **Citadella** fortress, at an elevation of 230m (760ft). It's well worth the Fts 300 admission price for the magnificent view from the ramparts – on a clear day you can trace the course of the Danube right through the city.

The Citadella, which was built by the Habsburgs in 1854 but never called upon to defend the city, contains a small hotel, restaurant, beer terrace and a few cases of historical artefacts. The summit is crowned by Budapest's own **Statue of Liberty** – a 14m (45ft) lady holding the palm of freedom who once had Soviet soldiers grouped at her feet – designed in 1947 for Admiral Horthy by **Zsigmond Kisfaludi Stróbl**.

From the top it's a pleasing stroll down to the **Gellért Hotel** (*see* panel, this page) with its own splendid baths; on the way down, any children with you will have fun on the longest **playground slides** they are ever likely to experience.

☆ *See* Map B–H2 ★

## VÁROSLIGET (CITY PARK)

This is Budapest's largest park, a square kilometre in size, offering plenty to do for all ages. First there is the **castle**, housing the **Hungarian Agricultural Museum** – the largest agricultural museum in Europe. The **Chapel of Ják**, part-modelled on the small chapel at Ják in western Hungary, is opposite. East of the castle, on the edge of the park, the **Transportation Museum** contains model railway locomotives and early cars; the museum's aviation and space section is housed close by in the **Petőfi Hall**, a rock and pop music venue.

Beyond the **Széchenyi Fürdő** (*see* panel) are the zoo, circus and amusement park. The **Municipal Circus** is directly opposite the baths. To its right is the **Vidámpark**, an amusement park that has some good old-fashioned rides – a log flume, dodgems, go-karts, wooden carousel and Ferris wheel among them – plus a Looping Star and the stomach-churning Ikarus. There are long-term plans for the amusement park to be resited. The **City Zoo** lies to the south of the circus and is known as much for its early 20th-century Art Nouveau buildings – these include the Elephant House, Palm House and Bird House – as for its inmates. The City Zoo includes a **Botanical Garden**.

---

**Széchenyi Fürdő**
The palatial Széchenyi Fürdő – one of Europe's largest public baths – is clearly identified by its series of copper domes. There are indoor and outdoor thermal baths, with mud treatments, jet massage and the whole range of spa experiences available. The temperature of the pools varies from 27°C to 38°C – you can even play chess as you bathe, using a floating cork board.

---

**Municipal Circus**
☎ 343 9630
🕐 performances at 10:00 on Sat and Sun, 15:00 on Wed, Thu and Fri, and 19:00 on Wed, Fri, Sat and Sun; closed in summer
💰 Fts 300–500

---

**Below:** *Széchenyi Fürdő is one of Europe's largest public baths.*

*See* Map B–D3  ★

### West and East

Pest's two great **railway stations**, the Nyugati (Western) and Keleti (Eastern), lie 3km (2 miles) apart. The **Western station**, facing Nyugati tér, was completed in 1877 by the Eiffel Company of Paris. It's a huge, cavernous structure of iron and glass covering 25,000m² (29,900 sq yd) that has rightly become a subject of conservation – in the early 1970s a train crashed right through the glass panel and came to rest by the tram stop outside. **Keleti**, Pest's other major railway edifice facing Baross tér, was built in 1884 and renovated in the 1980s.

**Opposite:** *The fine interior of the Great Synagogue.*
**Below:** *The 19th-century Központi Vásárcsarnok (Great Market Hall) near Liberty Bridge.*

## SZABADSÁG TÉR (INDEPENDENCE SQUARE)

This is one of Budapest's largest squares, laid out in 1897 on the site of a former barracks. It was here that **Count Lajos Batthyány**, prime minister of the independent Hungarian government, was shot after the Habsburgs had crushed the Hungarian insurrection in October 1849 – the spot has been marked since 1926 by an eternal flame.

On the square's southeast corner is the **Hungarian National Bank (MNB) building**, its façade adorned with reliefs depicting work. The Art Nouveau block next door is the heavily barricaded **US Embassy**, where Cardinal Mindszenty took refuge from 1956 until 1971; the **statue** on the green before it is of **Harry Hill Bandholtz**, an army general from the US peace-keeping force who prevented Romanians from looting the Hungarian National Museum in 1919.

Behind the embassy on Hold utca, half the block is taken up by Ödön Lechner's Art Nouveau former **Post Office Savings Bank**. Note the bees ascending to the roof – it could have been Gaudí-inspired. Across Hold utca is **Központi Vásárcsarnok**, a large indoor market hall from 1896.

At the north end of the square is the **Soviet Army memorial**, a rare reminder of 'Big Brother' still standing in the capital. Occupying the entire west side of Szabadság tér is the headquarters of **Hungarian Television (MTV)**, housed in the former **Stock Exchange** built in the early 1900s – note the twin towers in the style of an eastern temple.

# SZABADSÁG TÉR & JEWISH DISTRICT

| ✿ *See* Map B–G3 | ★ |
| --- | --- |

## JEWISH DISTRICT

The **VII district** east of Deák tér – known as **Erzsébet-város** or Elizabeth Town – has retained some of its prewar atmosphere, when it was the centre of Budapest's Jewish community. In the streets around Klauzál tér you will find synagogues and shops still at the heart of Jewish life, survivors from 1944–45 when some 70,000 Jewish people were walled up inside the ghetto.

Next to the **Great Syna-**

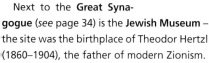

**gogue** (*see* page 34) is the **Jewish Museum** – the site was the birthplace of Theodor Hertzl (1860–1904), the father of modern Zionism.

The poignant **Holocaust Memorial** in adjacent Wesselényi utca takes the form of a metal tree, its leaves bearing the names of Hungarian Jewish families. Close by is a **monument to Carl Lutz**, a Swiss consul who supplied Jewish people with false wartime papers; the **Raoul Wallenberg Memorial Garden** is named after the Swedish diplomat who helped Jews to escape the Nazi clutches (*see* panel).

Other synagogues in the area include the Art Nouveau **Orthodox Synagogue** at Kazinczy utca 29–31 (currently under restoration), the **Moorish Conservative Synagogue** dating from 1872 at Rumbach Sebestyén utca 11, and the **Small Synagogue**, dating from 1364, at Táncsics Mihály utca 26.

**Raoul Wallenberg**
Raoul Wallenberg was the Swedish diplomat credited with saving the lives of thousands of Jews – estimates vary from 20,000 to 35,000 – in World War II by dispatching them to 'safe houses' or rescuing them from trains bound for the Auschwitz death camp. Wallenberg was 32 when he came to Budapest as an attaché in July 1944. Exactly what happened to Wallenberg when the Red Army liberated Budapest in 1945 is unclear; he is believed to have been arrested for espionage and to have died in a Soviet labour camp.

⚫ *See* Map B–D5 | ★

**Above:** *The elegant interior of Gerbeaud Coffee House.*

## HEART OF PEST

Pest is the **commercial** heart of Budapest, its grand buildings dating largely from the late 19th century. Much of interest to the visitor will be found in the **V district**, between the Danube and the **Kiskörút (the Little Ring Road)**, to the southeast of the Chain Bridge. A second semicircular 'layer' is created between Kiskörút and the **Nagykörút (the Great Ring Road)**, beyond which exploration leads you out to **Városliget**, the City Park (*see* page 29).

**Vörösmarty tér** is the tourist heart of Pest, its leafy expanse bounded by a mix of building styles. In its midst sits the poet **Mihály Vörösmarty** (1800–50); the statue's inscription, from his patriotic piece *Szósat* ('Appeal'), reads 'Be faithful to your country forever, oh Hungarians'. The statue, in Italian marble, wears a protective covering each winter to save it from cracking.

At the foot of the elegant white façade on the north side is the famous **Gerbeaud Coffee House** (*see* panel).

Heading south off Vörösmarty tér is Váci utca, Budapest's shopping hub. Marks and Spencer is here, along with boutiques, designer shops and big international names.

---

**Gerbeaud Coffee House**

In Vörösmarty tér you will find Gerbeaud Coffee House, its chairs and tables spilling onto the square in summer. The Swiss confectioner **Emile Gerbeaud** bought the patisserie in 1884 and turned it into a favoured venue of Budapest's coffee drinkers; the service nowadays may be a little slower, but the pastries, such as *mogyoró-trüffel torta* (hazelnut-truffle layer cake), are delicious.

---

See Map B–C3    ★

## VÍZIVÁROS (WATERTOWN)

The cluster of streets between Castle Hill and the river is the Víziváros, once a poor part of the city that was home to fishermen and craftsmen. The main artery of the Víziváros is **Fő utca**. On the south side of the adjoining Corvin tér is the former **Capuchin Church**, bearing the raven and ring symbols of King Matthias Corvinus – the square is named after him. Across the square is the neo-Classical façade of the **Budai Vigadó** concert hall, built between 1898 and 1900 – it is now home to the **Hungarian State Folk Ensemble**, founded in 1951.

Between Fő utca and the river on Szilágyi Dezső tér, the brightly tiled roof belongs to the late 19th-century **Calvinist Church**. Fő utca opens out into Batthyány tér, city terminus of the **HÉV** suburban railway. Dominating the square is **St Anne's Parish Church** (see page 35).

Two blocks further, on your left, is the former **Military Court of Justice** – an enormous brick building adjacent to Nagy Imre tér in which Nagy and other leaders of the 1956 Uprising were tried and executed two years later. Beyond is the thermal bath, the **Király Gyógy-fürdő** (see panel).

Crossing Ganz utca, you will reach **St Flórián's Chapel** (see page 35).

---

**Király Thermal Bath**
The distinctive **Király Gyógyfürdő** (Király thermal bath) has four small copper domes covering its octagonal pool. Decidedly Middle Eastern in appearance, it was first built by the Turks for their own garrison around 1580. Men and women may use the facilities on alternate days.
✉ Fő utca 84
☎ 202 3688
🕐 open to men and women on alternate days – men on Mon, Wed and Fri (09:00–21:00) and women on Tue, Thu (06:30–19:00) and Sat (06:30–13:00).

**Below:** *The Király Bath brings a touch of the Orient to Budapest.*

**Above:** *The Calvinist Church, Watertown.*

---

**The Matthias Well**
By the gateway into the Royal Palace's Lion Courtyard, guarded on each side by Fadrusz's pair of menacing lions, the Matthias Well with its bronze figures tells the story of the peasant girl **Szép Ilonka** (Fair Helen), who saw and fell in love with King Matthias while he was out hunting. On discovering his identity and realizing her hopes were in vain, she died of a broken heart. The fountain was created by Alajos Stróbl in 1904.

---

# Places of Worship

## Cave Church

The Cave Church on Gellért Hill, just north of the Gellért Hotel baths entrance, dates only from 1924, but has a fascinating history. Founded by monks of the long-established Pauline order, it was consecrated on Whit Sunday in 1926 and served them until the entire order was arrested by secret police on Easter Monday in 1951. A concrete wall blocking the chapel, erected by the communists, was removed on 27 August 1989 and the chapel returned to the order. The monastery, with its neo-Gothic turrets, is immediately behind the chapel.
✉ *Szent Gellért rkp 1*
☎ *385 1529*
🕓 *daily 09:00–20:00*

## Franciscan Church

This church is noted for its wall relief recounting the heroics of Baron Miklós Wesselényi, who rescued many Budapest citizens in his boat during the great flood of 13–16 March 1838; despite his efforts, more than 400 died.
✉ *Ferenciek tere 2*

## Great Synagogue

The Great Synagogue is the world's largest outside New York and can hold up to 3000 worshippers. It was completed in 1859 in Oriental-Byzantine style with patterned brickwork inspired by ancient Middle Eastern ruins. Extensive renovation work carried out in the 1990s was part-funded by a New York-based charity headed by the actor Tony Curtis, whose parents were Hungarian emigrants in the 1920s. The Jewish Museum on the site was the birthplace of Theodor Hertzl (1860–1904), the father of modern Zionism.

✉ Dohány utca 2–8
☎ 317 2754
🖳 www.great synagogue.hu
🕓 Jewish Museum Mon–Fri 10:00–15:00, Sun 10:00–13:00

## St Anne's Parish Church

This church dates from 1740–62, with twin copper spires each sporting a clock. The interior is gloriously Baroque, with the ceiling artwork extra special; the Italianate nave is an elongated octagon in shape.

✉ Batthyány tér 8
☎ 201 3404
🕓 for services only, Mon–Sat 06:45–09:00, 16:00–19:00; Sun 07:00–13:00

## St Flórián's Chapel

This bright yellow Baroque chapel was built in 1759–60 as a hospital chapel with a donation from Buda's master baker Antal Christ. Owned since 1920 by the Greek Catholic Church, the building was raised a metre and a half in 1936–37 to protect it from the flooding Danube.

✉ Fő utca

## St Michael's Premonstratensian Church

Destroyed during the Turkish Wars in 1541, this church on Margaret Island was rebuilt in 1930–31; the 15th-century bell was discovered among the roots of a walnut tree uprooted by a storm in 1914.

✉ Margaret Island

## University Church

The large Baroque University Church dates from the mid-

### Place of Rest

The expansive **Kerepesi Cemetery**, a short walk from Eastern railway station, is the final resting place of many prominent Hungarians. Pick up a map at the entrance on Fiumei út and find your way along paths among the splendid mausoleums and simple graves. Those interred here include former communist leader **János Kádár**; national heroes **Lajos Kossuth**, **Lajos Batthyány** and **Ferenc Deák**; the 'Nightingale of the Nation', **Lujza Blaha**; and the poet **Endre Ady**. Buried in a single large plot are many who lost their lives in the 1956 Uprising.

**Below:** *The Oriental dome of the Great Synagogue.*

### Stamps and Coins

Pest caters for philatelists and numismatists in two specialist collections – the small **Bélyegmúzeum (Stamp Museum)** at Hársfa utca 47, and the **Banknote and Coin Collection** at the Magyar Nemzeti Bank at Szabadság tér 8. The latter is an exhibition of Hungarian coins and banknotes down the ages, from a **denarius** of King Stephen I – Hungary's oldest coin – to banknotes showing millions of **forints** from the postwar period of massive inflation; there is a section on Transylvanian currency.

**Opposite:** *Mounted King Stephen is one of Budapest's finest statues.*
**Below:** *The view across Chain Bridge from the Pest side of the Danube.*

18th century; a copy of Poland's *Black Madonna of Czûstochowa* hangs above the altar.

⊠ *Eötvös Loránd utca 5–7*

**Other places of worship** on pages 16–17, 22, 25, 27, 29, 31 and 33.

## Museums

### Béla Bartók Museum

This museum on the edge of the Buda Hills pays tribute to the Hungarian-born pianist and composer. The house, where he lived from 1932 to 1940, contains a memorial room with original furniture and personal items – his folk art collection, letters and photos. The museum also contains a small exhibition of stamps, paintings and sculptures with Bartók as the theme.

⊠ *Csalán út 29*
🖥 *www.bartok museum.hu*
☎ *394 2100*
🕐 *Tue–Fri 10:00–17:00*

## Budapest History Museum

The **Budapesti Történeti Múzeum** (Budapest History Museum) in Wing E of the Royal Palace (*see pages 18–19*) traces 2000 years of Hungary's capital on three floors and features restored palace rooms from the 15th century. The Gothic Hall and Crypt contain statues of courtiers and religious figures discovered during excavations in 1974 – they're believed to have been discarded during 15th-century rebuilding work.

⊠ *Budavári Palota E*
☎ *375 7533*
📠 *355 9175*
✒ *btm@mail.btm.hu*
🖥 *www.vendegvaro.hu*
🕐 *Mar–Oct 10:00–18:00, Nov–Feb 10:00–16:00; closed Tue*

## Ethnography Museum

The neo-Renaissance museum was built in 1896 as the Supreme Court; it now houses a permanant exhibition,

'Folk Culture of the Hungarians', with its display of costumes.

✉ Kossuth Lajos tér 12
☎ 473 2400
📠 473 2401
🖥 www.neprajz.hu
🕑 Tue–Sun 10:00–18:00

## Ferenc Liszt Memorial Museum

This museum is housed in Liszt's former apartment of the Academy of Music he established. He lived here from 1881 until his death five years later. Most of the furniture is original; rare instruments displayed include Liszt's travelling keyboard and glass piano. There are also personal effects and manuscripts.

✉ Vörösmarty utca 35
☎ 322 9804
📠 413 1526
🖥 www.lisztmuseum.hu
🕑 Mon–Fri 10:00–18:00, Sat 09:00–17:00, closed from 1–20 Aug

## Golden Eagle Pharmacy Museum

Between the Holy Trinity Column by the

Matthias Church and the Royal Palace is the Golden Eagle Pharmacy Museum, housed in a building that dates from 1490. Founded in 1750, the pharmacy operated until 1913. Fascinating exhibits in the museum include ceramics, utensils, jars of antidotes, 2000-year-old 'mummy-head' powder for treating epilepsy, and an 18th-century distillation plant that the pharmacist also used for making brandy.

✉ Tárnok utca 18
☎ 375 9772
🕑 Tue–Sun 10:30–17:30

## Kodály Memorial Museum

For a glimpse into the life of another leading Hungarian composer, Zoltán Kodály (1882–1967), visit the Kodály Memorial Museum. The rooms in the neo-Renaissance mansion, one of four faded blocks surrounding the square, are much the same as they were when Kodály lived there, with pictures, manuscripts and other documents on display.

✉ Kodály körönd 1
☎ 352 7106
📠 322 9647
✉ kodaly.budapest@museum.hu
🖥 www.kodaly-inst.hu

**Above:** *The grand entrance to the Műcsarnok exhibition hall on Hősök tere.*

⊕ *Wed 10:00–16:00, Thu–Sat 10:00–18:00, Sun 10:00–14:00*

## Museum of Contemporary Art

**Kortárs Müvestzí Múzeum**, or Museum of Contemporary Art (*see page 19*), is better know as the Ludwig Museum after its founder, German industrialist Peter Ludwig. The museum, featuring the likes of Warhol, Lichtenstein and Hockney, is now housed at the contemporary **Palace of Arts**.
⊠ *Palace of Arts, Komor Marcel utca 1*
☎ *555 3444*
📠 *555 3458*
🖳 *info@ludwig museum.hu*
🖳 *www.ludwig museum.hu*
⊕ *Tue–Sun 10:00– 20:00; last Sat of each month 10:00–22:00*

## Museum of Fine Arts

**Szépmüvészeti Múzeum** (Museum of Fine Arts), completed in 1906, houses the nation's leading inter-national collection. There is a large gallery of Austrian and German works which includes giant canvases by Krafft (*The Crowning of Emperor Francis*) and Piloty (*Nero on the Burnt Ruins of Rome*). The 19th-century collection contains pieces by Gauguin, Monet, Renoir and Delacroix; there are also extensive Italian, Dutch and Flemish assemblies and a limited British representation with works by Reynolds, Gainsborough, Hoppner and Constable. European and American abstraction features in a basement gallery.
⊠ *Dózsa György út 41*
☎ *469 7100*
📠 *469 7171*
🖳 *szepmuveszeti. budapest@museum.hu*
🖳 *www.szep muveszeti.hu*
⊕ *Tue–Sun 10:00–17:30*

## National Széchenyi Library

**Országos Széchenyi Könyvtár** (National

Széchenyi Library) has its entrance in Lion Courtyard of the Royal Palace. Since 1802 it has accumulated more than two million books and countless newspapers, manuscripts and musical scores; a copy of every Hungarian-language publication from anywhere in the world finds its way here.

✉ Royal Palace, Wing F
☎ 224 3700
🖳 www.oszk.hu
🕓 Tue–Sun
10:00–18:00

## Petőfi Literature Museum

The **Petőfi Irodalmi Múzeum** (Petőfi Literature Museum) is housed in the 18th-century Károlyi Palace, itself recently refurbished. The museum contains the works and possessions of Sándor Petőfi and other noted Hungarian authors.

✉ Károlyi Mihaly utca 16
☎ 317 3611
📠 317 1722

🖳 www.plm.hu
🕓 Tue–Sun
10:00–18:00

## Vasarely Museum

The Vasarely Museum in Óbuda is dedicated to Hungary's best-known 20th-century artist, Victor Vasarely. He was a key exponent of Op Art, which creates interesting optical illusions. Through clever use of geometric designs the shapes appear to move on the canvas. The museum covers Vasarely's work from his early linear drawings to larger, more colourful pieces. Born in Pécs in 1908, Vasarely moved to Paris in 1930, where he lived until his death in 1997.

✉ Szentlékek tér 6–7, Óbuda
☎ 250 1540
📠 250 1540
🕓 Apr–Oct Tue–Sun 10:00–18:00, Nov–Mar Tue–Sun 10:00–17:00

**Other museums** on pages 14, 15, 21, 23, 26, 29 and 31.

---

**Tivadar Csontváry**

Kosztka Tivadar Csontváry (1853–1919) began his working life as a pharmacist and did not start painting until he was 41. He produced huge canvases of landscape scenes in Hungary, Italy, Dalmatia, Lebanon and Syria – among them *Ruins of the Greek Theatre at Taormina* and *Look Down on the Red Sea* – achieving greater recognition in the latter half of the 20th century than during his lifetime. Picasso's famous tribute to Csontváry was: 'And I thought that I was the only great painter of this century.' Much of his work is now displayed in the Csontváry Museum in Pécs.

---

**Below:** *The cupola of the Royal Palace, home to museums and the National Széchenyi Library.*

## Margaret Island

Heading north from Margaret Bridge, an extensive **sports centre** to your left offers tennis; there's a full-scale athletics stadium tucked behind the trees, beyond which you can hire a bike or four-wheel pedal carriage to explore the island. For the less energetic visitor, battery-operated cars can be rented by the hour or half-hour. With birdsong from the plane trees, the scent of freshly mown grass in the air and wooded parkland as far as the eye can see, it's hard to believe that you are in the centre of a bustling, modern city.

**Below:** *Communist-era statues in Szoborpark.*

# Parks
## The Statue Park

Ever wondered what happened to the statues of Lenin, Russian soldiers and proletarian heroes that adorned Budapest's streets not so long ago? At Szoborpark (Statue Park) are statues that were removed during the 1956 Uprising and others that were toppled from their plinths after the fall of communism in 1989.

✉ *10km (6 miles) southwest of the city centre*
☎ *424 7500*
🖥 *www.szoborpark.hu*
🕐 *daily 10:00–sunset*
🚌 *direct Statue Park bus from Deák tér*
💰 *Fts 2450 includes travel and admission*

## Margaret Island

Wooded Margaret Island, just over 2km (1.5 miles) long, is the city's playground, a haven for strollers and joggers and a retreat from the traffic along the river banks. Alight from the tram on Margaret Bridge and you have a fine perspective of the city; alternatively, the bus will take you right on to the island from the western train station.
🚌 *tram No. 4 or 6, bus 26*

## ACTIVITIES
### Sport and Recreation

Golf is played around Budapest. Try either the **Budapest Golf Park & Country Club** 35km (22 miles) to the north in the Danube Bend region, or otherwise the 18-hole **Pannon Golf & Country Club** 40km (25 miles) west at Alcsútdoboz-Máriavölgy; both are open from March to October.

Tennis centres are dotted about the city – two popular venues are the **Margaret Island Athletics Centre**, with four courts, and **Budapest Sports Club**, with 10 outdoor and two indoor courts.

Squash courts can be found at the **Budapest Marriott Hotel**, the **City Squash Club** and the **Lido Leisure Centre**. Tenpin bowling venues include the **MVA Bowling Centre**, the **Novotel**, and the **Hotel Stadion**. If you want to go horse riding, contact the **Budapest Riding Club** or the **Petneházy Riding School**.

It is possible to hire bicycles and there are some good cycle paths on Margaret Island, in the Városliget (City Park) and the Népliget, a park on the southeastern edge of the city centre.

**Golf**
**Budapest Golf Park & Country Club**
☎ 26 392 463
**Pannon Golf & Country Club**
☎ 22 594 200

**Tennis**
**Margaret Island Athletics Centre**
☎ 329 3406
**Budapest Sports Club**
✉ Szamos utca
☎ 213 5129, Pest XII

**Squash**
**Budapest Marriott Hotel**
✉ Apáczai Csere utca
☎ 266 7000
**City Squash Club**
✉ Marcibányi tér 13
☎ 325 0082, Buda II
**Lido Leisure Centre**
✉ Nánási út 67
☎ 250 2565, Buda III

**Tenpin Bowling**
**MVA Bowling Centre**
✉ Váci út 178 (Pest XIII)
☎ 465 1155
**Novotel**
✉ Alkotás utca 63–67 (Buda XII)
**Hotel Stadion**
✉ Ifjúság útja 1–3.

**Horse Riding**
**Budapest Riding Club**
✉ Kerepesi út 7
☎ 313 5210, Pest VIII
**Petneházy Riding School**
✉ Feketefej utca 2–4
☎ 397 5048, Buda II

**Left:** *The large outdoor public bath at Széchenyi Fürdő.*

Away from the city, there are more sporting choices. Hungary is an **equestrian** nation and abundant opportunities exist in all parts of the country both for trail riding and for tutoring novices and advanced riders alike. The greatest concentration of equestrian facilities can be found around Lake Balaton and on the Great Plain.

Lake Balaton offers an unrivalled variety of outdoor pursuits. **Dinghy sailing** has been popular there for well over a century; conditions are ideally suited and on summer weekends the sails of hundreds of yachts can be seen on the lake. Dinghies can be hired by the day or for an hour or two – as can boards for **windsurfing**.

You can also hire a bicycle and pedal off along the edge of Lake Balaton; some 240km (149 miles) of **cycle tracks** are now open, linking the many towns and villages all around the lake. There is plenty of scope for cycling in Hungary – over stiff gradients in the Northern Uplands, across less demanding terrain in Transdanubia, and over the vast and often windy flat expanse of the Great Plain.

**Fishing** is a big attraction in the early and late summer, for the *fogas* (pike-perch) for which Balaton is known, and also for carp – both can weigh up to about 10kg (22lb). The Tisza River in the east of the country is another prime angling location.

**Taking the Reins**

Hungarians' enthusiasm for equestrian sports extends to carriage driving, and they are among the world's best. Schools throughout the country provide single, two- and four-in-hand tuition where you can learn the rudiments of the sport; within a week you can be harnessing up a pair of horses and driving yourself. As Hungary's equestrian centre, Hortobágy is a good place to advance your horse-riding techniques. Traditional gypsy caravans provide an alternative way to holiday in equestrian company; well schooled in horse care, you can set out to explore the Great Plain.

## Alternative Budapest

Budapest and its surrounds have plenty to offer when you have done the traditional sights. The **House of Terror** is in the former headquarters of the Hungarian fascists and communist secret police (✉ Andrássy utca 60, ☻ Tue–Fri 10:00–18:00; Sat–Sun 10:00–20:00) and serves as a memorial to totalitarian terror in all its forms. Over the years many left-wing activists and communists were beaten and tortured within its walls. Now the rooms tell a grim story from World War II through the 1956 Revolution to 1989, when the last Soviet troops left Hungarian soil.

For a bathing experience with a difference, head for the wonderful **thermal bath** of the Art Nouveau **Gellért**, grand old lady among Budapest's hotels. It opened in 1918 on a prime site by the Szabadság bridge. With its high columns, majolica tiles and lion water-spouts, the thermal bath is one of the wonders of Budapest. There are also outdoor swimming and thermal pools.

If you've an interest in Hungarian history, the large **Kerepesi Cemetery**, a short walk from the Keleti (East) railway station, is the final resting place of many Hungarian worthies. Pick up a map at the entrance and explore among the mausoleums and simple graves. Among those buried here are the former communist leader János Kádár; national heroes Lajos Kossuth, Lajos Batthyány and Ferenc Deák; the 'Nightingale of the Nation', Lujza Blaha; and the poet Endre Ady.

> **Caving on High**
> You can go caving in the northern Buda Hills – on organized tours through spectacular stalactite caves. The **Pálvölgy** cave system (Szépvölgyi út 162), Hungary's third largest, is noted for its stalactites and bat colony. The **Szemlő hegy** caves (Pusztaszeri út 35) have stalactites, stalagmites and crystal formations that look like bunches of grapes. The caves are about a kilometre apart and can be reached by taking the HÉV train from Batthyány tér to Szépvölgyi út and then bus 65.

**Opposite:** *Practising bicycle skills on Heroes' Square.*
**Below**: *This small post van is ideal for negotiating the city's narrow streets.*

## Fun for Children

Budapest has plenty for children to enjoy. **Vidámpark** amusement park, the **Municipal Circus** and **Zoo**, all located in the Városliget (City Park), have their young fans and there are also plenty of activities for children on Margaret Island.

To the left of the Western Station in Pest the **Palace of Wonders Interactive Scientific Playhouse** provides a hands-on environment that makes science fun for youngsters up to 16 years; weird and wonderful exhibits and activities keep them entertained. The **Budapest Puppet Theatre** has classic fairytales on offer, but unfortunately only in Hungarian.

Head for the Budapest Hills aboard a train staffed by 10- to 14-year-olds – the narrow-gauge **Gyermekvasút (Children's Railway)**, which will take you about 12km (8 miles) into the hills from the summit of Széchenyi-hegy. You can hike into the woods from stations en route – the fourth stop, János-hegy, is the highest point in and around Budapest at 527m (1729ft). A separate cog-wheel railway takes you to Széchenyi-hegy from its lower station near the circular tower of the Budapest Hotel, itself just a short walk from Moszkva tér.

---

**Palace of Wonders Interactive Scientific Playhouse**
✉ Váci út 19
☎ 350 6397
🕐 Mon–Fri 09:00–17:00, Sat–Sun 10:00–18:00; closed Mon Jan–Apr
💰 Fts 450, children Fts 400

**Budapest Puppet Theatre**
✉ Andrássy út 69
☎ 321 5200
🕐 booking office daily 09:00–18:00
📧 bubab@hdsnet.hu

**Gyermekvasút (Children's Railway)**
✉ Széchenyi-hegy
☎ 397 5392
🖥 www.gyermek vasut.hu
🕐 year-round, except Mon from Sep–Apr; trains run 09:00–19:00 in summer, 09:00–17:00 in winter

**Below:** *Traditional Russian Matryoshka dolls make unlikely if popular souvenirs of Budapest.*

## Walking Tours
### The Castle District

Take the Budavári Sikló (funicular railway) from Clark Adam tér by the Chain Bridge and from its upper station turn to savour the view of Pest on the opposite side of the Danube.

Head north with the **Royal Palace** behind you and at cobbled Disz tér, with its war-damaged former **Ministry of Defence** building, go left on to the cannon-flanked promenade of Tóth Árpád sétány, which looks across to the Buda Hills.

Leave the promenade at Szentháromság utca, heading towards the bulk of the **Matthias Church**, and at the **statue** of Hussar general **András Hadik**, turn left into Úri utca where passageways in the fine old town houses lead through to hidden courtyards.

Turn right into Dárda utca and left into Országház utca, paralleling Úri utca towards Kapisztran tér – numbers 18 to 22 Országház utca well illustrate how the Castle District would have looked in medieval times.

On the square of Kapisztrán tér, the **Mary Magdalene Tower** is all that's left of a large 13th-century church destroyed in World War II. Across the square in a former barracks is the **Military History Museum**.

Go right on Peterman Biro utca past the **National Archives** building into Bécsi kapu tér and the **Vienna Gate** within the city walls. By the **Lutheran Church**, head up Fortuna utca into Hess András tér with the **Hilton Hotel**.

Turn left on the corner of the Hilton opposite the Matthias Church and go behind the building on to the **Fisherman's Bastion**, with its pointed turrets. Climb the steps and walk along it for some of the best views of the city. At its end, pass the fine

**Above:** *Budapest's Castle District is a fascinating part of the city to explore on foot.*

---

**The Castle District Walking Tour**
**Location:** Map B–C4
**Distance:** about 2 km (1.25 miles)
**Duration:** 2 hours
**Start and Finish:** upper station of the funicular

---

**Above:** *The Holocaust Memorial takes the form of a metal tree, its leaves bearing the names of Holocaust victims.*

equestrian statue of King Stephen I and walk up the slope with the Matthias Church on your right. Turn left at the top near the **Holy Trinity Column** and walk back to the funicular. Alternatively, a path zigzags from the Fisherman's Bastion down the hill towards the river.

## Jewish District Walking Tour

Midway between Deák tér and Astoria on the red metro line is the landmark **Great Synagogue**, at the heart of **Erzsebétváros** (Elizabeth Town) and focal point of Budapest's Jewish community – it's well worth a look inside.

Alongside it is a remnant of the brick wall that imprisoned 70,000 Jewish people in the World War II ghetto, and up the stairs to the left of the main entrance the **Jewish Museum**, with its many artefacts and room dedicated to the Holocaust.

In a courtyard just a short way along Wesselényi utca, to the side of the Great Synagogue, is the **Holocaust Memorial** in the form of a willow tree. A little further along, left down Rumbach utca, is the **monument to Carl Lutz** on the corner of Dob utca.

Further along Rumbach utca, on the right, is the yellow and rust-coloured **Moorish Conservative Synagogue**, now closed. At the end of the street, turn right into Király utca and at number 13 enter the series of connected courtyards between residential buildings typical of the Jewish district.

**The Jewish District Walking Tour**
**Location:** Map B–E5
**Distance:** about 2 km (1.25 miles)
**Duration:** 2 hours
**Start:** Great Synagogue
**Finish:** Wesselényi utca

They take you back on to Dob utca – turn left here and at Kazinczy utca head right to the Art Nouveau **Orthodox Synagogue**, currently under restoration, with its strict Hanna kosher restaurant. Go through the courtyard and emerge on to Dob utca again.

Go right into Klauzál tér, the largest square of the Jewish district, with the **Vásárcsarnok** (market hall) – one of several steel-spanned market halls in the city dating from the 1890s.

Leave the square at its southern corner by Nagy Diófa utca and turn right on to the first crossing street, Wesselényi utca, back towards the Great Synagogue. At number 13 is the **Judaica Art Gallery**, with Jewish-related books, art and religious items.

## Budapest's Architecture Walking Tour

**Batthyány tér**, a broad riverside square where the HÉV suburban line from Szentendre and the red metro line meet, is the start of a walk taking in a varied selection of interesting buildings close to the Danube.

The twin-spired church dominating Batthyány tér is the mid-18th-century **St Anne's Parish Church** with its glorious Baroque interior. Passing to its right along Fő utca, you will soon reach an ecclesiastical contrast, the 19th-century **Calvinist Church** with its brightly coloured roof.

About 200 metres further on your right is the neo-Classical **Budai Vigadó** concert hall, completed in 1900 and facing

**Budapest's Architecture Walking Tour**
**Location:** Map B–C4
**Distance:** about 2.8 km (1.8 miles)
**Duration:** 2.5 hours
**Start:** Batthyany tér
**Finish:** Parliament Building

**Below:** *The eastern influence is evident in the Oriental-Byzantine architecture of Budapest's Great Synagogue. The patterned brickwork was inspired by ancient Middle East ruins.*

**Go Walkabout**
Guided walks with English-language commentary show visitors the best of Budapest. They explore the architectural styles of the **Castle District**, from the Royal Palace to the Vienna Gate (departing from Matthias Church) and leave the Café Gerbeaud on Vörösmarty tér, taking in sights on the **Pest** side of the river. Companies include:
**Budapest Zigzag**
☎ 06 20 979 6105
**Absolute Walking Tours**
☎ 266 8777
**Budapest Walks**
☎ 340 4232
**Paul Street Tours**
☎ 06 20 958 2545.
Other walking tours focus on aspects of **Jewish Budapest**.

**Below:** *Contrasting architectural styles come together in the Castle District.*

the former **Capuchin Church** – with the raven and ring symbols of King Matthias Corvinus – across Corvin tér.

Just past the church, head left down Halász utca for good views across the river and turn right along the river past the modern **French Institute** of 1992. Rejoin Fő utca and turn left across the **Chain Bridge**.

The bridge crosses to Roosevelt tér and facing you is the distinctive Art Nouveau **Four Seasons Gresham Palace Hotel**, which is housed in the century-old former Gresham Life Assurance Company building.

Continuing direction on the opposite side of Roosevelt tér, exit by Zrínyi utca and turn left into Október 6 utca. This leads on to **Szabadság tér** (Independence Square), with a fascinating variety of buildings.

On the right is the **Hungarian National Bank** building, with wall reliefs depicting work in all its forms, and the **US Embassy**. On Hold utca behind the embassy, you'll see Ödön Lechner's former **Post Office Savings Bank** building with its giant bees ascending to the roof.

On your left as you cross the square is the former **Stock Exchange** building with its distinctive Oriental-inspired towers from 1900 now housing the **Hungarian TV (MTV)** headquarters. Leave by Vécsey utca to finish the walk opposite the fine riverside **Parliament Building**, styled by Imre Steindl on the Houses of Parliament in London.

## Organized Tours

**Budatours** offers a two-hour city tour with headphone commentary in 16 languages, including English; tours depart from Andrássy út 3. **Cityrama** will collect you from your hotel for its 4.5-hour city tour which departs from near the Parliament building. **Queeny Bus** includes a Parliament visit on its four-hour city tour departing from Szent István tér. The city tours follow a broadly similar route, covering the Castle District, the Royal Castle and the Citadel on Gellért Hill on the Buda side, and tracking through Pest, taking in the Parliament building, the Opera House and St Stephen's Basilica to Heroes' Square.

**Jewish Heritage in Budapest** has a 2.5-hour walking tour of the largest central European Jewish diaspora, departing daily except Saturday. Book tickets in advance.

Other excursions available from the main operators include a tour of the Parliament building, the Statue Park, Szentendre and the Danube Bend, the Baroque chateau at Gödöllő, dinner in the Buda Hills, Danube River cruises, and a relaxing day at a spa on Margaret Island.

*Above: Budapest's yellow trams offer the most enjoyable way of seeing the city, with great river views.*

<u>City Tours</u>
**Budatours**
✉ Andrássy út 2
☎ 374 7050, 374 7060, or 374 7070 (Pest V)
**Cityrama**
✉ Báthory utca 22
☎ 302 4382 (Pest V)
**Queeny Bus**
✉ Törökbálinti út 28
☎ 247 7159 (Buda XI)

<u>Jewish Budapest Tours</u>
**Chosen Tours**
✉ Pagony utca 40
☎ 355 2202 (Buda XII)
**Cityrama**
✉ Báthory utca 22
☎ 302 4382 (Pest V)
**Jewish Heritage in Budapest**
☎ 317 2754

## SHOPPING
## Shops and Markets

South off Vörösmarty tér is **Váci utca**, the capital's shopping hub. Marks and Spencer is here, along with boutiques, designer shops and some big international names like Lancôme, Estée Lauder and Clarins. If you're looking for souvenirs, the whole range is available – laceware, costumed dolls, hand-painted eggs and colourful embroidered children's dresses, napkins and tablecloths that make great

**Above:** *Westend City Center is open until late. With more than 400 shops, it's one of Europe's largest retail malls.*
**Below:** *Hungarian lace work with its brightly coloured flowers can be found in tablecloths, napkins and other household adornments.*

gifts. Packed with shops and the occasional hotel, Váci utca reaches all the way to Vámház kòrút by Szabadság hid (Liberty Bridge) – this was the extent of Pest in medieval times; by the late 18th century it had become the fashionable shopping district it is today.

Alternatively, soon after leaving Vörösmarty tér, take Kristóf tér on the left, with its appealing fisher girl statue, to **Szervita tér**, dominated by the 18th-century Servite Church. Note the fine gable mosaic depicting Hungaria opposite, above the Dr Jeans shop at No. 3; the contemporary looking Rózsavölgyi building at No. 5 dates from 1912, the inspiration of Béla Lajtha.

From Szervita tér, **Petőfi Sándor utca** – one of 17 streets and squares in Budapest named after Hungary's greatest poet – heads south a block east of Váci utca with more shops and the main post office at No 13; traffic-free streets link the two shop ping zones. Head west along Pilvax köz to the colourful square of Kamermayer Károly tér, with the green Pest County Hall and vast pink and gold 18th-century City Hall, stretching into the distance down Városház utca. Károly Kamermayer (1829–97) was Budapest's first mayor. His statue adorns the square; the narrow streets leading off it contain small antique shops. Back on Petőfi Sándor utca, the dark and forbidding Párizsi Udvar arcade next to the Ferenciek tere underpass contains a real rarity – a hologram shop.

For retail therapy, stick to the Pest side of the river. You will find many of Budapest's most expensive shops on and around the pedestrianized Váci utca, Petőfi Sándor utca, Régiposta utca, Haris köz, Párizsi utca and Kigyó utca, but there are numerous other stores and specialist shops lining Pest's wide boulevards. While tourists throng Váci utca and offshoot streets, locals tend to favour the ring road from the Western station towards the Petőfi Bridge.

Next to the Western station, on Váci út (not to be confused with Váci utca) is the **Westend City Center**, one of Budapest's last major projects of the 1990s. It has one of Europe's largest shopping centres – open until late, and full of familiar and less familiar names. The site includes the new upmarket Hilton Westend Hotel, with a tethered balloon that provides great city views.

Shopping malls outside the centre of town include the **Duna Plaza**, the **Pólus Center**, and **Arkád**.

## Some Shopping Malls

**Duna Plaza**
✉ Váci út 178
(Pest XIII)
☎ 465 1666
🕐 Mon–Fri
10:00–21:00, Sat–Sun
10:00–19:00
Ⓜ Gyöngyösi utca

**Pólus Center**
✉ Szentmihályi út 131
(Pest XV)
☎ 414 2145
🕐 Mon–Fri
10:00–20:00, Sat–Sun
10:00–19:00
🚌 shuttle bus from
Keleti pályaudvar

**Arkád**
✉ Örs Vezér tér 25
(Pest X)
☎ 434 8200
🕐 Mon–Fri
10:00–21:00, Sat–Sun
10:00–19:00
Ⓜ Örs Vezér tér

**Westend City Center**
✉ Váci út 1–3
☎ 238 7777
Ⓜ Nyugati Pályaudvar

**Below:** *Hungarian craft work makes an excellent souvenir.*

## Some Like it Hot

The long strands of dark red and orange paprikas you see hanging out to dry are the very trademark of Hungarian cuisine, yet paprika is not Hungarian in origin. Paprika is said by some to have been brought back from the Americas by Columbus; others say it arrived with the Turkish invaders. It is now popular both as a pickled or fresh vegetable, and also in powdered form for the seasoning of dishes.

**Below:** *Fruit and vegetables for sale at one of Budapest's colourful indoor markets.*
**Bottom right:** *Paprika is a staple of Hungarian cooking.*

The **Központi Vásárcsarnok** (the Great Market Hall) on Vámház körút, on the Pest side of Szabadság híd (Liberty Bridge), was one of five similarly styled indoor market buildings constructed in the late 19th century. The hall is on three levels – you enter by the middle one, packed with meats and vegetables. Head downstairs for fish – there are tanks of live creatures at the back – and up to the gallery with its profusion of lacework, embroidery and other souvenir items. The Fakanál restaurant on the gallery will feed you cheaply and well.

## What to Buy

What do you buy in Hungary? You could go for porcelain (Herend and Zsolnay are big names here), antiques, folk art, costumed dolls, painted eggs, books and CDs, to name but a few. **Bookshops** include Irok Boltja (the Writer's Bookshop), at Andrássy út 45 (Pest VI), and Bestsellers, at Október 6 utca 11 (Pest V). Belure Bookstation (closed Monday), at Thököly út 18 (Pest VII) is a new bookshop with English titles, while Király Books, at Fő utca 79 (Buda II) specializes in English and French books.

For a good selection of **music** CDs, you could try Rózsavölgyi Zeneműbolt, located

at Szervita tér 5 (Pest V) or Fotex, close by at Szervita tér 2. Fono Budai Zenéház, at Sziregova utca 3 (Buda XI) is a folk and world music shop.

Though you will find **antique** shops all over the city, collectors strapped for time should head for the Pest V district, with a large concentration of outlets in Falk Miksa utca, near Margaret Bridge; the southern part of Váci utca; or Kossuth Lajos utca. Try Bélvarosi Aukcióház, Váci utca 36 (Pest V); Antik Udvar, Szent

István körút 1 (Pest V); Darius Antiques, Falk Miksa utca 24–26 (Pest V); and Enterieur Antikvitás, Országház utca 2 (Buda I).

**Above:** *Pest Central Market Hall is good for browsing.*

The world-famous Herend and Zsolnay **porcelain** factories both have retail outlets in the Pest V district of Budapest – Herend is at József nádor tér 11 and Kigyó utca 3, while the Zsolnay shops can be found at Ferenciek tere 11 and Kigyó utca 4. The leading porcelain brands can be found in Haas and Czjzek, Bajcsy Zsilinszky út 23 (Pest VI).

Having no doubt acquainted yourself with some fine **wines** during your stay, you will want to take some home – good options include Bortarsasag (The Budapest Wine Society), Batthyány utca 59 (Buda I) with outlets at Szilágyi E fasor 121, Gábor Árun utca 74–78, and Ráday utca 7; La Boutique des Vins, József Attila utca 12 (Pest V), and House of Hungarian Wines, Szentháromság tér 6 (Buda I).

### Good for Browsing
Váci utca alters character south of Ferenciek tere. On your left, the large cream building at No. 38 is a former officers' casino, now a bank headquarters. The shops here are more interesting and include a number selling **antiques**. Among the shops is the immense bulk of Budapest City Hall. Right opposite, you can pause at No. 65 for a cuppa at the **1000 Tea** shop. Towards Szabadság hid (Liberty Bridge), cafés and restaurants have terraces on the pedestrianized street.

**Right:** *Four Seasons Gresham Palace, one of several deluxe hotels along the Danube.*

### Where to Stay

Long before the fall of the Iron Curtain, Budapest offered its visitors a choice of hotel accommodation unrivalled by any other city in eastern Europe. International names – such as Hyatt, Ramada, InterContinental, Hilton and Forum – were complemented by properties of Hungary's own Danubius and Hungar Hotels chains. During the 1990s the hotel range expanded further with the addition of many three-star 'panzió' (pension) properties, popular with city-break visitors seeking less expensive but nonetheless comfortable accommodation. Choose a property in one of Budapest's outlying areas, linked to the centre by bus or tram – or the HÉV suburban rail services – and it will work out a lot cheaper than opting for a room with a view across the Danube. A nice area is the Buda Hills, where you can escape the bustle of the city though still with good public transport connections. Note that generally there are fewer hotels on the Buda side of the river.

## WHERE TO STAY
## Budapest

### • *LUXURY*
### Budapest Hilton

(Map B–B4)
Situated in the heart of Buda's old Castle District, the five-star Budapest Hilton with its copper-coloured glass façade offers its guests all the amenities and remarkable Danube views. The hotel also incorporates part of a Dominican church and monastery.
⊠ *Hess András tér 1–3, 1014 Budapest (Buda I),*
☎ *889 6600,*
📠 *889 6644,*
🖲 *info.budapest @hilton.com*
🖥 *www.hilton.com*

### Corinthia
### Aquincum

A modern five-star hotel facing Margaret Island, close to the site of the former Roman garrison. It offers reliable access to the city centre by suburban railway.
⊠ *Árpád Fejedelem útja 94, 1036 Budapest (Óbuda III),*
☎ *436 4100,*
📠 *436 4156,*
🖲 *reservation@ aqu.hu*
🖥 *www.corinthia hotels.com*

### Corinthia Grand
### Hotel Royal

(Map B–F3)
This superb five-star is arguably the best hotel in town. With

its soaring central atrium, the Royal is luxurious and really knows how to turn on the style.

✉ *Erzsébet körút 43–49, 1073 Budapest (Pest VII),*
☎ *479 4920,*
📠 *479 4921,*
✈ *royalresidence@ corinthia.hu*
🖥 *www.corinthia hotels.com*

## Danubius Gellért

(Map B–D6)
A Budapest landmark near Szabadság híd (Liberty Bridge), the four-star Gellért has welcomed the rich and famous for more than 80 years. The hotel boasts an elegant façade and also a splendid thermal pool, which guests may use free. (*See also* panel, page 28.)

✉ *Szent Gellért tér 1, 1111 Budapest (Pest XI),*
☎ *889 5500,*
📠 *889 5505,*
✈ *gellert.reservation@ danubiusgroup.com*
🖥 *www.danubius hotels.com*

## Danubius Grand Margitsziget

(Map C–C3)
The former Ramada Grand, built more than a century ago, is situated on leafy Margaret Island, a short distance upriver from the city centre. Guests can share the comprehensive spa facilities of the adjacent Danubius Thermal Margitsziget.

✉ *Margitsziget, 1138 Budapest (Margaret Island XIII),*
☎ *889 4700,*
📠 *889 4939,*
✈ *resind@margit sziget.danubius group.com*
🖥 *www.danubius hotels.com*

## Four Seasons Gresham Palace

(Map B–D4)
Former life assurance building that's now one of the top hotels in Budapest. Art Nouveau in style, it has a prime position by the Chain Bridge.

✉ *Roosevelt tér 5–6, 1051 Budapest (Pest V),*
☎ *268 6000,*
📠 *268 5000,*
🖥 *www.fourseasons. com*

## Kempinski Corvinus

(Map B–D4)
This is a strikingly modern and centrally located five-star hotel close to the Váci utca shopping area. It is hugely expensive, but it does offer the very highest standards of service and cuisine.

✉ *Erzsébet tér 7–8, 1051 Budapest (Pest V),* ☎ *429 3777,*
📠 *429 4777,*
✈ *hotel.corvinus@ kempinski.com*
🖥 *www.kempinski- budapest.com*

## • MID-RANGE

### Best Western Hotel Art (Map B–E6)

Restored hotel with 32 rooms and lots of character, located in a quiet backstreet of central Pest.

✉ *Királyi Pál utca 12, 1053 Budapest (Pest V),* ☎ *266 2166,*
📠 *266 2170,*
🖥 *http://book. bestwestern.com*

**Best Western Grand Hungaria** (Map B–F5)
Large 500-room four-star hotel on a main thoroughfare within easy distance of Keleti (east) station. The restaurant has live gypsy music and an ice cream parlour.
⊠ Rákóczi út 90, 1074 Budapest (Pest VII),
☎ 889 4400,
📠 889 4411,
🖱 grandhungaria. reservation@danubius group.com
🖥 www.danubius hotels.com

**Budapest** (Map B–A3)
Cylinder-shaped tower in an attractive setting beneath the Buda Hills. It is situated close to the Fogaskerekű cogwheel railway. There are good views from all the rooms of either the city or the hills.
⊠ Szilágyi E. fasor 47, 1026 Budapest (Buda II), ☎ 889 4200,
📠 889 4203,
🖱 budapest.reservation @danubiusgroup.com
🖥 www.danubius hotels.com

**Carlton Budapest** (Map B–C4)
This modern three-star hotel is situated near the Chain Bridge at the foot of Castle Hill.
⊠ Apor Péter utca 3, 1011 Budapest (Buda I),
☎ 224 0999,
📠 224 0990,
🖱 carltonhotel@ t-online.hu
🖥 www.carlton hotel.hu

**Danubius Astoria** (Map B–E5)
Traditional four-star in late 19th-century style, right in the centre of Pest. It was built on the site of Budapest's former medieval walls and is well known for its fine coffee house.
⊠ Kossuth Lajos utca 19, 1053 Budapest (Pest V),
☎ 889 6000,
📠 889 6091,
🖱 astoria.reservation@ danubiusgroup.com
🖥 www.danubius hotels.com

**Danubius Flamenco** (Map B–A6)
A modern hotel in the residential district on the Buda side, away from the city-centre bustle, but convenient for the sights.
⊠ Tas vezér utca, 1113 Budapest (Buda XI),
☎ 889 5600,
📠 889 5651,
🖱 flamenco. reservation@ danubiusgroup.com
🖥 www.danubius hotels.com

**Danubius Health Spa Resort Margitsziget** (Map C–C2)
Four-star thermal spa hotel of the Danubius Group in which huge sums have been invested. Thermal pools and a wide range of health and fitness facilities at one of Hungary's leading spa properties.
⊠ Margitsziget, 1138 Budapest (Margaret Island XIII),
☎ 889 4700,
📠 889 4988,
🖱 resind@ margitsziget. danubiusgroup.com
🖥 www.danubius hotels.com

## Danubius Thermal Hotel Helia

(Map C–C4)

This large modern four-star hotel faces Margaret Island across the Danube. There are lots of spa-related facilities, including indoor pool, thermal baths and Finnish sauna. There are also rooms for handicapped guests.

✉ *Kárpát utca 62–64, 1133 Budapest (Pest XIII),* ☎ *889 5800,*
💲 *889 5801,*
📠 *helia@danubius group.com*
🖥 *www.danubius hotels.com*

## Erzsébet (Map B–E5)

Three-star hotel very handily placed for Váci utca shopping street. Its appealing restaurant serves Hungarian specialities; there is also a pub dispensing draught beer.

✉ *Károlyi Mihály utca 11–15, 1053 Budapest (Pest V),*
☎ *889 3700,*
💲 *889 3763,*
📠 *erzsebet.reservation @danubiusgroup.com*

🖥 *www.danubius hotels.com*

## Ibis Budapest Centrum (Map B–E6)

Situated on a fashionable pedestrianized street, close to cafés and bars.

✉ *Ráday utca 6, 1094 Budapest (Pest IX),*
☎ *456 4100,*
💲 *456 4116,*
🖥 *www.accorhotels. com*

## K&K Opera

(Map B–E4)

Opera buffs and art lovers will appreciate this Austrian-managed four-star hotel – it is just 50 metres from the Opera House, with works of art in every bedroom.

✉ *Révay utca 24, 1065 Budapest (Pest VI),*
☎ *269 0222,*
💲 *269 0230,*
📠 *kk.hotel.opera@ kkhotels.hu*
🖥 *www.kkhotels.com*

## Mercure Nemzeti

(Map B–F5)

A centrally located Art Nouveau-style three-star hotel on Blaha Lujza tér in Pest. Built in the 1880s, the 76-room boutique-style hotel has a pleasant turn-of-the-century ambience.

✉ *József körút 4, 1088 Budapest (Pest VIII),* ☎ *477 2000,*
💲 *477 2001,*
📠 *H1686@accor.com*
🖥 *www.mercure.com*

## Stadion (Map B–H3)

This modern 365-room three-star hotel is situated a bit out of town, near the Népstadion sports stadium, but close to the metro. The hotel has its own six-lane tenpin bowling alley.

✉ *Ifjúság útja 1–3, 1148 Budapest (Pest XIV),* ☎ *889 5200,*
💲 *889 5252,*
📠 *stadion.reservation @danubiusgroup.com*
🖥 *www.danubius hotels.com*

## Taverna (Map B–D5)

If shopping is your reason to be in Budapest, this modern four-star hotel will certainly satisfy you – it is situated smack in the pedestrianized shopping area of Váci utca. The 222-room hotel has its own bowling alley.

✉ *Váci utca 20, 1052 Budapest (Pest V),*
☎ *485 3100,*
✆ *485 3111,*
✆ *hotel@hotel taverna.hu*
🖥 *www.taverna.hu*

## • *BUDGET*

## Beatrix Panzió

(Map B–A3)

This small family-run pension has 22 rooms and sits at the foot of the Buda Hills.

✉ *Széher út 3, 1021 Budapest (Buda II),*
☎ *275 0550,*
✆ *394 3730,*
✆ *beatrix@hotel. t-online.hu*
🖥 *www.beatrix hotel.hu*

## Best Western

**Orion** (Map B–C5)

This three-star hotel is located on the Buda side of the Elizabeth Bridge.

✉ *Döbrentei utca 13, 1013 Budapest (Buda I),*
☎ *356 8583,*

✆ *375 5418,*
🖥 *http://book. bestwestern.com*

## City Hotel Mátyás

(Map B–D6)

A central three-star hotel near Erzsébet híd (Elizabeth Bridge), situated above the well-known Mátyás Pince restaurant, in which guests take their breakfast. Most of the rooms have views of the Danube and Buda Castle.

✉ *Március 15 tér 7, 1056 Budapest (Pest V),*
☎ *338 4711,*
✆ *317 9086,*
✆ *matyas@taverna.hu*
🖥 *www.taverna.hu*

## City Hotel Pilvax

(Map B–D5)

This modern 36-room hotel is well located close to Deák tér, where the three metro lines intersect.

✉ *Pilvax koz 1–3, 1052 Budapest (Pest V),*
☎ *266 7660,*
✆ *317 6396,*
✆ *pilvax@taverna.hu*
🖥 *www.taverna.hu*

## City Hotel Ring

(Map B–D2)

This three-star sister to the City Hotel Mátyás is situated close to the Nyugati (Western) rail station. It offers simple but good city-centre accommodation at an affordable price.

✉ *Szent István körút 22, 1137 Budapest (Pest XIII),*
☎ *340 5450,*
✆ *340 4884,*
✆ *ring@taverna.hu*
🖥 *www.taverna.hu*

## Gold Hotel Panzió

(Map B–I1)

This comfortable 22-room pension is just a short bus ride from the Mexikói metro terminus.

✉ *Pándorfalu utca 15, 1142 Budapest (Pest XIV),*
☎ & ✆ *252 0470 or 251 6282,*
✆ *panzio@gold hotel.hu*
🖥 *www.goldhotel.hu*

## Ibis Emke Hotel

(Map B–F4)

This three-star hotel has a good location

just off Blaha Lujza tér in Pest.

✉ Akácfa utca 1–3, 1072 Budapest (Pest VII),

☎ 478 3050,

✆ 478 3055,

🖥 www.ibishotel.com

### Kalocsa Panzió

(Map B–I4)

A comfortable hotel at an affordable price in the east of the city.

✉ Kalocsai utca 85, 1141 Budapest (Pest XIV),

☎ 221 4721

✆ 363 238.

### Panzió Molnár

(Map B–A6)

Attractively designed pension with 23 rooms. It is situated high on the Buda side of the city, a 15-minute bus ride from downtown Pest.

✉ Fodor utca 143, 1124 Budapest (Buda XII), ☎ 395 1873.

## Esztergom

• *MID-RANGE*

### Hotel Esztergom

(Map D–A1)

Modern three-star hotel where Little

Danube meets its big sister.

✉ Prímás sziget, 2500 Esztergom,

☎ 33 412 555,

✆ 33 412 853,

✎ info@hotel-esztergom.hu

🖥 www.hotel-esztergom.hu

## Lake Balaton

• *MID-RANGE*

### Annabella

(Map E–E2)

Located on the northern shore of Lake Balaton and one of the area's largest hotels, the Arabella has 388 rooms and a pool deck. It is great for families.

✉ Deák Ferenc utca 25, 8230 Balatonfüred,

☎ 87 889 400,

✆ 87 889 412,

✎ sales.balatonfured @danubiusgroup.com

🖥 www.danubius hotels.com

## Szentendre

• *BUDGET*

### Bükkös Panzio

(Map D–C2)

This charming, inexpensive 16-room pen-

sion is located in the centre of town.

✉ Bükkös-part 16, 2000 Szentendre,

☎ 26 312 021,

✆ 26 310 782

## Visegrád

• *MID-RANGE*

### Silvanus (Map D–C1)

A three-star hotel near the hilltop citadel. It offers great views over the Danube River.

✉ Fekete-Hegy, 2025 Visegrád,

☎ 26 398 311,

✆ 26 597 516,

✎ info@hotel silvanus.hu

🖥 www.hotel silvanus.hu

## Zebegény

• *MID-RANGE*

### Kenderes

(Map D–B1)

This delightful modern 24-room three-star hotel is situated on the Danube's north bank.

✉ Dózsa György út 26, 2627 Zebegény,

☎ 27 373 444,

✆ 27 373 444,

✎ kenderes@ dunaweb.hu

## EATING OUT
## What to Eat

Hungary is not the best place to be in the world for vegetarian visitors or those who are on a strict diet. But it does offer a wide variety of interesting and exciting ethnic flavours to sharpen the jaded palate.

*Reggeli* **(breakfast)** can sometimes consist of just a roll and a cup or two of good strong coffee, or otherwise it can include a full-blown plate of meat, cheese and eggs, and may on occasion even be helped down by an early morning *pálinka*, the powerful local brandy.

Though *ebéd* **(lunch)** is traditionally the main meal of the day for Hungarians, you can choose to dine just as copiously in the **evening *(vácsora)*.** You will never be left wanting more – Hungarian food is solid and filling, the ample dishes often traceable back to peasant origins.

Hungarians are a nation of great **meat** eaters, with pork being the most popular meat of choice. But other meats – beef, wild boar, veal, venison, chicken, turkey, pheasant, duck and goose – can all be found gracing menus, too. Small dumpling-sized **noodles**, called *galuska* often accompany the meal.

**Fish** is plentiful, especially around Lake Balaton; the local *fogas* (pike-perch) is a tasty delicacy, and carp, pike and trout also abound. Speciality fish dishes include *paprikás ponty* (carp in paprika sauce) and *pisztráng tejszín martásban* (trout baked in cream).

The word *martás* is Hungarian for **sauce**, of which there are quite a few to accompany your meat or fish; some of the most popular of the sauces are *bormartás* (wine sauce), *meggymartás* (cherry sauce), *fokhagymás martás* (garlic sauce) and *gombamartás* (mushroom sauce).

**Paprika** is widely used and is a common ingredient in many Hungarian meals. It comes in several degrees of piquancy, from mild to hot – whatever your feelings about the spice, it adds a quintessentially Hungarian character to any meal.

But first, the starter. Hungary is rich in *levesek* **(soups)** of all kinds, and you are bound to sample some *gulyásleves* (*see* panel, page 60). At Lake Balaton and along the Tisza River around Szeged, the emphasis switches to **fish** and *halászlé* – a spicy, paprika-laden fish stew with giant lumps of pike-perch and carp; it's often cooked in a mini-cauldron and can be taken as a main course.

**Above:** *Paprika is one of the key ingredients of Hungarian cuisine.*
**Opposite:** *Spicy goulash soup is delicious.*

### King of Wines

Louis XIV was unequivocal in his praise of **Tokaj wine**, calling it 'the wine of kings and the king of wines'. Others to sing its praises included Voltaire, Beethoven, Goethe and Schubert. The wine, golden in colour, owes its distinctive qualities to the volcanic soil that permits a later harvest, when the grapes are sweeter – these are **Aszú grapes**. Tokaj wine is rated in **puttony**, the number of Aszú baskets added to the regular grapes that regulate its sweetness; there are also drier varieties.

Other soups include *jókai bableves* (bean soup with smoked meat) and *újházi tyúk-leves* (chicken soup with noodles) – also **cold soups** that go down well in summer, like *meggyleves* (cold sour cherry soup).

When it comes to **dessert**, the Hungarian *rétes* (strudel) is well worth saving space for; it is filled either with apple, sour cherry or cottage cheese. Also delicious is the *gundel palacsinta*, a flambéed pancake with nuts and raisins covered in a chocolate and rum sauce.

## What to Drink

Hungarian **wines** can be of excellent quality, the best-known among them being *Tokaj* (see panel, this page). Some outstanding white wines are produced on the northern slopes above Lake Balaton and you are sure to try *Egri Bikavér*, the deep red 'Bull's Blood' produced from several varieties of grape.

**Above:** *Hungarian wines are of excellent quality.*
**Opposite:** *Gerbeaud Coffee House is an institution not to be missed.*

## Where to Eat

Dining out in Budapest never presents a problem. Choose Hungarian or international cuisine, or else something from the wide variety of ethnic eateries: French, Greek, Indian, Italian, Mediterranean, Jewish, or Asian. Then decide on which side of the river you intend to spend the evening – Pest offers the wider selection, but Buda rewards those prepared to travel a bit further with some really excellent venues. The restaurants of the touristy Castle District tend to be more expensive, but they are rarely disappointing. The word for restaurant is *étterem*; a *vendéglő* is often more rustic in style and cheaper, while a *bisztró* explains itself.

Coffee houses were a second home to writers and artists, poets and actors, singers and journalists – the atmospheric cafés that sprang up in Budapest from the 1900s to the 1930s and earned the Hungarian capital a reputation as 'the city of coffee houses'. Nowadays elderly Hungarian ladies and visitors to the city pass time pleasantly in those same coffee shops that survived the upheavals of World War II and its aftermath. Along with the coffee – a double espresso will set you up for the day – come all manner of cakes and pastries to further sweeten your day in Budapest.

### Coffee and Cake

The *cukrászda* (Hungarian patisserie) caters for the Hungarians' sweet tooth and is often part of a larger chandelier-decked coffee house where you can gorge on sticky strudel, well-filled pancakes or anything from the inevitably impressive display of cakes and pastries. Get your tongue round a *dobostorta* (chocolate and cream cake with a topping of brown sugar and caramel). To follow, there's strong espresso coffee (ask for milk to dilute), maybe cappuccino and usually tea. **Gerbeaud**, founded in 1884, is Budapest's best-known coffee house (see page 32).

## Budapest

### • *LUXURY*
### Chez Daniel

The best creative
French cuisine to be
found in Budapest,
with the menu
changing daily. Highly
popular – booking is
recommended.
⊠ *Szív utca 32,*
☎ *302 4039 (Pest VI).*

### Corvinus

Top-notch Hungarian
and international
offerings in the Bistro
Jardin. The wonderful
Hungarian buffet on
Wednesday evenings
is a bargain.
⊠ *Erzsébet tér 7–8,*
☎ *429 3777 (Pest V).*

### Gambrinus

Dine well in this
showpiece restaurant
in the heart of Pest.
⊠ *Hotel Taverna, Váci
utca 20,* ☎ *485 3100
(Pest V).*

### Gundel

Hungary's most
famous restaurant
was founded in
1894. It is extremely
expensive and smart
dress is *de rigueur*.
⊠ *Állatkerti körút 2,*
☎ *468 4040 (PestXIV).*

### Kehli Vendéglő,

More than a century
old, this courtyard
restaurant was reput-
edly a favourite of

the noted Hungarian writer and gourmet Gyula Krúdy. Some way from downtown, it is located in a square of Óbuda.

✉ Mókus utca 22,
☎ 368 0613 (Buda III).

### Képíró

French-inspired menu; also Hungarian and international cuisine, served in stylish surroundings on two floors.

✉ Képíró utca 3,
☎ 266 0430 (Pest V).

### Király

Classy Hungarian-style restaurant in the Castle District.

✉ Táncsics Mihaly utca 25,
☎ 212 8565 (Buda I).

### Le Jardin de Paris

French restaurant with more than a dash of Hungarian, between the Castle District and the river.

✉ Fő utca 20,
☎ 201 0047 (Buda I).

### Mátyás Pince

This traditional restaurant is popular

with large groups. Nevertheless, it gives good service – and at acceptable prices.

✉ Marcius 15 tér 7,
☎ 266 8008 (Pest V).

### Remíz

Named after the nearby tram depot, this restaurant offers diners an interesting mix of Hungarian and international dishes, plus an extensive wine list on a varied menu.

✉ Budakeszi út 5,
☎ 275 1396 (Buda II).

### Vadrózsa

A small Baroque villa houses this highly pricey Hungarian speciality restaurant with its two dining rooms on Rózsadomb, the

**Above:** *Wine from Tokaj is Hungary's finest.*
**Opposite:** *A sidewalk café in Pest.*

---

**Upscale Dining**
**Gundel**, next door to the Zoo, is Hungary's best-known restaurant, where the accent is very much on traditional Hungarian recipes. It was founded by Károly Gundel in 1894 and is known both for its excellent cuisine and the oil paintings adorning the walls of its colonnaded interior (for key to the artists, see the back of the menu). A favourite on the menu is the *palacsinta* (Gundel pancake), a crêpe filled with flambéed chocolate sauce and crushed walnuts. After dinner to the accompaniment of a gypsy ensemble, diners may be invited to look over the extensive wine cellar.

Hill of Roses. Dine well to a soft piano accompaniment.
✉ *Pentelei Molnár utca 15,*
☎ *326 5817 (Buda II).*

• **MID-RANGE**

### Apostolok

The neo-Gothic interior gives a church-like feel to this century-old restaurant which is located in the centre of Pest. The food is largely traditional Hungarian.
✉ *Kigyó utca 4–6,*
☎ *318 3559 (Pest V).*

### Aranybárány

It means 'golden lamb' and not surprisingly lamb is the speciality here. The ambience is Hungarian with lots of dark wood.
✉ *Harmincad utca 4,*
☎ *267 0213 (Pest V).*

### Bagolyvár

The name of this restaurant literally means 'owl's castle'; this is the cosy lower-brow sister to next-door Gundel (*see* under Luxury) and priced accordingly,

but with high standards to match.
✉ *Állatkerti út 2,* ☎ *468 3110 (Pest XIV).*

### Bombay Palace

A member of the international chain, highly regarded for its flavours of India – and newly renovated.
✉ *Andrássy út 44,*
☎ *332 8363 (Pest VI).*

### Café Pierrot

This became Budapest's first privately owned café in 1982 and is still going strong in the city's Castle District, offering good-quality Hungarian fare to the accompaniment of piano music.
✉ *Fortuna utca 14,*
☎ *375 6971 (Buda I).*

### Carmel Pince

This non-kosher restaurant uses traditional Jewish recipes and also serves both Hungarian and international fare. It is adjacent to the Orthodox synagogue.
✉ *Kazinczy utca 31,*
☎ *342 4585 (Pest VII).*

### Cascade

This restaurant offers a good seafood and vegetarian selection in the Buda environs.
✉ *Szarvas Gábor út 8,*
☎ *275 2115 (Buda XII).*

### Dionysos

Greek restaurant on the Pest riverfront decked out as a Greek village square.
✉ *Belgrád rakpart 16,*
☎ *318 1222 (Pest V).*

### Karpátia

Hungarian and Transylvanian fare is served here, in historic and sophisticated surroundings. The restaurant has an outside terrace; live gypsy music adds to the occasion.
✉ *Ferenciek tere 7–8,*
☎ *317 3596 (Pest V).*

### Pest Buda Vendéglő

Ethnic Hungarian fare served in gracious surroundings in Buda's Castle District.
✉ *Fortuna utca 3, 1014 Budapest,*
☎ *212 5880 (Buda I).*

## Replay Café

A terraced restaurant which has its heart firmly in the Mediterranean.
✉ Fehér Hajó utca 12–14, ☎ 266 8333.

## Seoul House

Authentic Korean recipes give this restaurant an edge over most of the other Asian restaurants in Budapest.
✉ Fő utca 8, ☎ 201 9607 (Buda I).

## Szeged

This tastefully furnished eating house, with delicious fish specialities, is located to the south of Gellért Hill.
✉ Bartók Béla út 1, ☎ 209 1668 (Buda XI).

## Trombitás

The restaurant's genuine Hungarian ambience is an ideal setting for the nightly folk dancing display. The food here is in the best Hungarian traditions, and the location is very convenient – right on Moszkva tér.
✉ Retek utca 12, ☎ 212 3154 (Buda II).

## Udvarház

Terrace dining in the Buda Hills with a dramatic overview of the city. Folklore show most evenings.
✉ Hármashatárhegy út 2, ☎ 388 8780 (Buda III).

## Új Sipos Halászkert

Stylish venue in the heart of Óbuda.
✉ Fő tér 6, ☎ 388 8745 (Buda III).

## • BUDGET
## Fu Hao

A large restaurant with Chinese specialities from all parts of that country; the buffet offers 20 dishes daily.
✉ Dózsa György út 76, ☎ 342 7368 (Pest VII).

## Okay Italia

Lively Italian restaurant with outstanding pasta and pizza, situated near the Nyugati (Western) railway station. There is another branch close by.
✉ Szent István körút 20, ☎ 349 2991 (Pest XIII).
✉ Nyugati tér 6, ☎ 332 6960.

## Tabáni Gösser

Small restaurant offering Hungarian and international fare on the western side of Castle Hill.
✉ Attila út 19, ☎ 375 9482 (Buda I).

## • COFFEE HOUSES
## Angelika

Romantic café in a historic building by St Anne's Parish Church. Some rooms are partitioned off by velvet drapes.
✉ Batthyany tér 7, ☎ 212 3784 (Buda I).

## Astoria Café Mirror

The four-star Danubius Astoria is one of Budapest's grand late 19th to early 20th-century hotels and the rather grand café with its leather-upholstered chairs well recaptures the spirit and ambience of a century ago.

✉ *Kossuth Lajos utca 19*, ☎ *889 6000 (Pest V).*

## Augustz Cukrászda

Family-run business, dating from 1870, with a courtyard attached. Excellent range of pastries.
✉ *Kossuth Lajos utca 14–16*, ☎ *337 6379 (Pest V).*

## Café Mai Mano

If you're exploring the theatre district off Andrássy út, pop into this quirky little café in the Hungarian House of Photography building with its comfy benches and tiled tables.
✉ *Nagymező utca 20*, ☎ *265 5642 (Pest VI).*

## Café Mozart

Themed café where coffee is served by costumed wenches to a background of the great composer's music.
✉ *Erzsébet körút 36*, ☎ *352 0664 (Pest VI).*

## Café Pierrot

The Pierrot was estab-lished back in the communist-ruled early 1980s as Budapest's first privately owned cafe. It is a comfort-able place in which to linger – and tuck away some local specialities if you're peckish – and there's live piano music in the evening.
✉ *Fortuna utca 14*, ☎ *375 6971 (Buda I).*

## Centrál Kávéház

A well-known literary café that has been restored to its early 19th-century ele-gance, now a restaurant-cum-coffee shop all in one that stays open till late.
✉ *Károlyi Mihály utca 9*, ☎ *266 2110 (Pest V).*

## Gerbeaud

This is without ques-tion Budapest's best-known coffee shop, founded by the Swiss confectioner Emile Gerbeaud in 1884, in the same building in which is it still housed today. The main cof-fee shop is always well populated by tourists.
✉ *Vörösmarty tér 7*, ☎ *429 9000 (Pest V).*

## Lukács

Splendidly restored late 19th-century café with a bright interior and some excellent gilt-work – plus piano music on some weekdays.
✉ *Andrássy út 70*, ☎ *302 8747 (Pest VI).*

## Muvész

This legendary chandeliered coffee house is situated almost opposite the Opera House. It serves great pastries and is strong on traditional ambience.
✉ *Andrássy út 29*, ☎ *352 1337 (Pest VI).*

## Ruszwurm

An appealing coffee house in Buda's Castle District – ideally situ-ated for a break from sightseeing. They have been serving coffee here since the 1820s and Princess Elizabeth ('Sissy') is said to have been among its former patrons.

✉ *Szentháromság utca 7,* ☎ *375 5284 (Buda I).*

### Zsolnay Café

If coffee and cake is your delight, don't miss the Zsolnay Café. More than 100 types of cake and 12 coffee varieties are served here, in the heart of Pest's shopping district.

✉ *Vaci utca 20,* ☎ *485 3110 (Pest V).*

## Esztergom
### • MID-RANGE
### Prímás Pince

Beneath the road to the basilica, it boasts a high vaulted ceiling. The food is good, too.

✉ *Szent István tér 4, 2500 Esztergom,* ☎ *33 400 063.*

## Szentendre
### • MID-RANGE
### Promenade

Wonderfully presented meals in a fabulous outdoor setting.

✉ *Futó utca 4, Dunakorzó, 2000 Szentendre,* ☎ *26 312 626.*

## Visegrád
### • MID-RANGE
### Gulyás Csárda

As the name implies, goulash and many other Magyar dishes are served in this appealing village-centre restaurant.

✉ *Nagy Lajos Király utca 4, 2025 Visegrád,* ☎ *26 398 329.*

### Renaissance

This restaurant exudes medieval ambience with its costumed waiters and wenches, its clay plates and goblets. You can don a cardboard crown and feast like a king or queen.

✉ *Fő utca 11, 2025 Visegrád,* ☎ *26 398 081.*

## Lake Balaton Northern Shore
### • MID-RANGE
### Blaha Lujza

Restaurant of centrally located three-star hotel.

✉ *Blaha Lujza utca 4, 8231 Balatonfüred,* ☎ *87 581 210.*

### Tűzkert

A wide selection of oven dishes is on offer at this restaurant (open April–October).

✉ *Batthyány utca 15, 8237 Tihany,* ☎/✆ *87 438 060.*

## Bakony Hills
### • MID-RANGE
### Elephant Bistro

Italian-themed eatery with a pleasant terrace, on the town hall square.

✉ *Varoshaz tér, Veszprém.*

### Vázsonykő

Try *lecsó galuskával*, a Hungarian ragout with egg noodles. Delicious!

✉ *Temető út 2, Nagyvázsony,* ☎ *88 264 344.*

## Lake Balaton Southern Shore
### • MID-RANGE
### Oreghalasz

Inexpensive restaurant with a strong Hungarian theme.

✉ *Zamardi utca 10, Siófok,* ☎ *84 350 313.*

## ENTERTAINMENT
### Nightlife

You should never be stuck for ideas on how to make the most of your Budapest visit. When you've had your fill of sightseeing, there is a vast choice of things to do – from opera, ballet, classical concerts and folklore shows to jazz, discos, nightclubs and casinos – there is even a puppet theatre. Pick up a copy of the *Where Budapest* or *Budapest In Your Pocket*, for the latest information and listings of what's happening all over town.

## Opera, Theatre, Dance and Music

Try to find time for a night at the **opera**; even for non-opera buffs, a visit to the **State Opera House** is a worthwhile experience, if only to enjoy the building's sumptuous interior; the Opera House also stages performances of the State Ballet company. Other venues staging opera are the **Erkel Theatre** (also used by the State Opera company) and **Duna Palota** (Duna Palace), which stages classical performances of all kinds.

**Some Venues**
**State Opera House**
✉ Andrássy út 22
☎ 353 0170, Pest VI
**Erkel Theatre**
✉ Köztársaság tér 30
☎ 333 0540, Pest VIII
**Duna Palota (Duna Palace)**
✉ Zrínyi utca 5
☎ 235 5500, Pest V
**Nemzeti Szinház (National Theatre)**
✉ Bajon Gizi Park
☎ 476 6868, Pest XI
**Thália Theatre**
✉ Nagymező utca 22–24
☎ 312 4230, Pest VI
**Merlin Theatre**
✉ Gerlóczy utca 4
☎ 317 9338, Pest V
**The Budapesti Operett Szinház**
✉ Nagymező utca 19
☎ 353 2172, Pest VI
**Liszt Music Academy**
✉ Liszt Ferenc tér 8
☎ 342 0179, Pest VI

Other theatre venues include **Nemzeti Szinház (National Theatre)**, the **Thália Theatre**, the **Merlin Theatre** and the **Budapesti Operett Szinház**. The **Castle Theatre** (Várszínház) near the Royal Palace is a former Carmelite church; it was converted into a theatre in 1784 and renovated in the 1970s.

For lovers of classical music, the **Liszt Music Academy** is Budapest's leading concert venue, with nightly performances in its splendid Great Hall; concerts are also given in the **Budapest Congress Centre**.

For light classics, check out the **Pest Concert Hall**. The **Béla Bartók Memorial House** has regular performances of the composer's work; the **Comedy Theatre** is good for operetta performances.

Organ recitals are given in churches, among them the **Matthias Church** in Buda's

**More Venues**
**Budapest Congress Centre**
⊠ Jagelló út 1–3
☎ 372 5700, Buda XII
**Pest Concert Hall (Pesti Vigadó)**
⊠ Vigadó tér 2
☎ 327 4322, Pest V
**Béla Bartók Memorial House**
⊠ Csalán út 29
☎ 394 2100, Buda II
**Comedy Theatre**
⊠ Szent István körút 14
☎ 329 2340, Pest XIII
**Bábszínház**
⊠ Andrássy út 69
☎ 321 5200, Pest VI
**Buda Concert Hall (Budai Vigadó)**
⊠ Corvin tér
☎ 201 3766, Buda I
**International Buda Stage**
⊠ Tárogató út 2–4
☎ 391 2525, Buda II
**Great Synagogue**
⊠ Dohány utca 2–8
☎ 317 2754, Pest VII
**Petőfi Hall**
⊠ Városliget, City Park
☎ 363 3730, Pest XIV

**Opposite:** *The stylish exterior of the State Opera House.*
**Left:** *The Castle Theatre (Várszínház) was formerly a church.*

# ENTERTAINMENT

Castle District (*see* page 16); **St Stephen's Basilica** (*see* page 22); and the **Great Synagogue** (*see* page 34).

Performances of traditional Hungarian folk music, often with full gypsy orchestra, are given in the **Duna Palota** (*see* page 70); in the **Bábszínház**, and in the **Buda Concert Hall**. The latter venue also hosts the Hungarian State Ensemble of folk dancers and gypsy orchestra from April to October each year. Musical performances with an international flavour take place at the **International Buda Stage**; Jewish music and culture is regularly celebrated in the **Great Synagogue**.

Rock and jazz clubs are dotted about Budapest. A leading concert venue is

the **Petőfi Hall** in Városliget. There's live jazz at the basement **Jazz Café**, the **Merlin Jazz Club** and the **Dokk-Jazz Bistro**, and live Latin at the **Franklin Trocadero**. For out and out disco, try the underground **Made Inn** or the highly popular **Bahnhof**, located by the side of the West railway station. If a quieter night out is more to your taste, **Piaf** is a small nightclub near Oktogon metro station, in the traditional style with a small dance floor.

Folk music is very much alive in Hungary and the *táncház* (dance house) is where it all happens. You'll find them in Budapest and towns around Hungary. The range of instruments used in traditional folk music is wide – *cimbalom* (an unusual stringed instrument played with a stick), violin, zither, bagpipe, hurdy-gurdy and lute among them. You could learn one or two of the lively Hungarian dances while you're there. Folk music should not be confused with gypsy music, which stems from the *verbunkos* (soldiers' recruitment tunes) and is performed in restaurants throughout the land.

## Cinema

Hungary has made a major contribution to the world of celluloid. Sir Alexander Korda, a founder of the British film industry, produced *The Scarlet Pimpernel*, written by Hungarian aristocrat Baroness Orczy. George Cukor was a noted Hollywood film producer; actors and actresses with Hungarian roots include Béla Lugosi, Leslie Howard, Tony Curtis and Zsa Zsa Gabor.

Other prominent Hungarians include world-famous conductor Sir George Solti, Ervin Bossanyi, designer of the Bossanyi stained-glass windows in Canterbury Cathedral, and the eminent gastronomist Egon Ronay.

**Above:** *Traditional folk music is much in evidence, with the opportunity to learn a Hungarian dance or two.*
**Opposite:** *The strains of gypsy-inspired music are often within earshot.*

**Above:** *Wearers of embroidered costumes strike a festive pose.*

## Festivals

Budapest is one of Europe's top festival cities, with an amazing array of cultural and fun happenings taking place in the time between the two really big events on the cultural calendar – the **Spring Festival** and **Autumn Festival**.

Both festivals offer an assorted programme of music, dance and drama, involving international artists and using Budapest's wide range of performance venues – from the splendid **State Opera House** to the small **Puppet Theatre**. The Spring Festival goes on in late March and the Autumn Festival in October.

In between are the **Budapest Early Music Forum** in May–June, **Ferencváros Summer Festival** in the Ferencváros district in June–July, the **Festival of Folk Art** at the Royal Castle and the **Budapest Summer Music Festival** in August, and also **Budapest Music Weeks** in September–October.

The **Budapest Fair** in late June has a strong dance content, while pop culture takes over in the **Sziget (Island) Festival** held on Budapest's Danube islands during August. In late August, the colourful **Budapest Street Carnival** ends with a street party in Heroes' Square.

In late summer, going into September there's the **Jewish Summer Festival**, with various concerts, films and exhibitions, and also the **Budafok Champagne and Wine Festival**, with wine cellar visits and folk dancing displays.

## Spectator Sports

Budapest's large sporting centre, situated roughly midway between the Városliget (City Park) and Kerepesi Cemetery, is focused on the **Puskás Ferenc Stadion** (the former Népstadion), a 68,000-seat stadium that stages international football matches and rock concerts. Other venues on the site include the **Kisstadion** and the indoor **Budapest Arena**.

The **FTC Stadium** of leading Budapest soccer club Ferencváros is at ⌧ Üllői út 129, opposite the Népliget (People's Park) on the main highway that leads southeast to the airport – the club's distinctive green and white colours are evident throughout Ferencváros, an inner-city suburb.

## Gambling

Budapest has a number of **casinos**, most demanding a smart-casual dress code. Among them are the hotel-based Casino Budapest Hilton, Las Vegas Casino, the Tropicana Casino and the Várkert Casino in a former pump-house beside the Danube.

**Below:** *The Várkert Casino below the Royal Palace has an exclusive feel with its mosaic arches.*

**Opposite:** *Budapest bar with a penchant for the past.*

## Gay Budapest

Gay venues include the following:

**Action Bar**
✉ Magyar utca 42
☎ 266 9148

**Angyal Bar**
✉ Szovetség utca 33
☎ 351 6490

**Capella**
✉ Belgrád rakpart 23
☎ 328 6231

**Café Eklektika**
✉ Semmelweis utca 21
☎ 266 3054

**Mystery Bar**
✉ Nagysándor József utca 3
☎ 312 1436

**Gellért** and **Király Baths** both have a gay clientele.

## Pubs and Clubs

### Arcadia

Lively place with star turns and go-go girls, open late at weekends. Has a cocktail bar and garden.
✉ Fehérvári út 120
☎ 206 1225
🕘 Mon–Thu 11:00–24:00, Fri 11:00–05:00, Sat 21:00–05:00
💰 free for girls up to 23:00

### Fáklya Club

Underground club, a hit with ravers keen on their fix of techno and rock. Good if you like your music loud.
✉ Csengery utca 68
☎ 332 4580
🕘 22:00–06:00

### Fat Mo's

Air-conditioned basement bar with plenty of beers on tap. Seating limited, but room at the bar.
✉ Nyáry Pál utca 11
☎ 267 3199
🕘 Mon–Tue 12:00–02:00, Wed 12:00–03:00, Thu–Fri 12:00–04:00, Sat 18:00–04:00, Sun 18:00–02:00
💰 free entry

### Fregatt

English-style pub near Elizabeth Bridge, where you'll bump into expats looking to down a few pints.
✉ Molnár utca 26
☎ 318 9997
🕘 Mon–Fri 15:00–01:00, Sat–Sun 17:0–01:00

### Incognito

Trendy bar that's good for jazz and cocktails. It gets packed in summer, when the clientele doubles up with the Café Mediterranean across the road.
✉ Liszt Ferenc tér 3
☎ 267 0239
🕘 Mon–Fri 10:00–24:00, Sat–Sun 12:00–24:00

### Janis' Pub

It takes its name from blues singer Janis Joplin and is within easy distance of leading Pest hotels. Live music most nights.
✉ Király Pál utca 8
☎ 266 2619
🕘 Mon–Thu 16:00–02:00, Fri–Sat 16:00–03:00

### John Bull Pub

Brits feeling homesick will definitely take to Budapest's first English-style pub. There's even a dartboard at this franchised venue.

⊠ Révay utca 6
☎ 269 4471
🕓 12:00–23:00 daily

### Mask Music Club

Soul, funk, acid jazz and hip-hop provide for a mixed clientele at this compact club with a high reputation for its pizza.

⊠ Kertész utca 33
☎ 267 8616
🕓 Mon–Fri 11:00–03:00, Sat 18:00–04:00

### Old Man's Music Pub

Relaxed atmosphere that's strong on blues, soul, funk and country music – there's live music every night.

⊠ Akácfa utca 13
☎ 322 7645
🕓 15:00–03:00; live music from 21:00
💰 free entry

### Universum

Café-cum-club in shopping street. The daytime crowd becomes a clubbing clientele in their 20s who bop to the DJ sounds.

⊠ Vaci utca 33
🕓 Mon–Sat 11:00–04:00, Sun 12:00–03:00

### Wig Wam

Live music rock club with blues and country; '80s and '90s music on Thu, rock parties till dawn on weekends.

⊠ Fehervari út 202
☎ 208 5569
🕓 20:00–05:00; concerts start at 22:00

### Zöld Pardon

Open-air venue with a large bar, dance floor, well-priced drinks; chairs to lounge in.

⊠ Near Petőfi bridge, on the Buda side
🖥 www.zp.hu
🕓 daily 09:00–06:00; concerts from 20:00; DJ from 22:30
💰 free entry

**Above:** *Sunbathing by the shore of the lake in the resort of Balatonudvari.*

## EXCURSIONS
### Lake Balaton

Known as the 'Hungarian sea', Balaton is Europe's largest freshwater lake outside Scandinavia. It is the playground of Hungary and neighbouring countries of central Europe.

The Tihany Peninsula, jutting far out into the lake, fully merits its popularity. The crowning glory of **Tihany** is the Baroque twin-spired **Abbey Church**, built in 1754 on the site of a Benedictine abbey founded in 1055 – the crypt containing the tomb of King Andrew I can be visited beneath the church. The **Benedictine Abbey Museum** contains a history of the church and a room dedicated to Charles IV, the last Hungarian king.

From the church, the Pisky sétány promenade leads past the **Open-air Museum**, featuring restored 18th-century houses, and the **Dolls Museum** to Echo Hill. By throwing your voice at the church wall you can hear the echo – if you're lucky, a party of schoolchildren may already be testing their vocal chords.

Northeast of Tihany is **Balatonfüred**, regarded as the 'capital' of Lake Balaton. It's the oldest and largest resort on the north shore of the lake, where the well-to-do of the 19th century built their villas.

Close to Balatonfüred heading towards the north are peaceful **Csopak**, noted for its wine-tasting cellars, and **Balatonalmádi** a spa town since 1877, with the northern shore's longest beach and buildings of red Permian sandstone.

---

**Getting Around Balaton**

Railway lines link the resorts of both the northern and southern shores with Budapest – useful if you want to travel back and forth across the lake on the MAHART boats and don't have to return to your starting point. In high summer, a service operates the length of the lake between Balatonkenese and Keszthely – the trip takes five hours and stops are made on both sides of the lake.

# LAKE BALATON

After the relaxed and spacious resorts of the north shore, **Siófok** – Balaton's largest resort by a long way – assails the senses with its wall-to-wall slot arcades, fast-food restaurants and cheap souvenir stands along Petőfi sétány to the east of the canal. But a glance across this particular street will reveal an altogether more illustrious past, with enormous villas, most well past their prime, tucked away behind the trees.

Though rather too brash for some, Siófok is a pleasant enough spot in which to spend an afternoon. At No. 5 Kálmán Imre sétány is the **Imre Kálmán Museum**, dedicated to the noted composer of operettas (1882–1953), who was born in Siófok in a house on the site – his works include *Countess Mariza* and *Queen of the Csárdás*. A short way down Hock köz brings you to Siófok's impressive wooden **Water Tower** on Szabadsag tér, built in 1912.

West of Siófok, there's a broad similarity about the sequence of small resorts, most prefixed by 'Balaton-', that line the southern shoreline across the rail tracks from Route 71 which circuits the lake.

At the lake's western end, a marshy region known as **Kis-Balaton** (Small Balaton) supports at least 100 bird species, of which cormorants, herons and bee-eaters are among the most common. There are two good bird hides for enthusiasts, located at Kányavár Island and Pap Island.

**Lake Balaton**
**Location:** Map E
**Distance from Budapest:** 80km
(50 miles)

### Hévíz

Hévíz is Hungary's best-known spa. It sits by Europe's largest thermal lake where, in mineral-rich water at a constant 30°C (86°F), bathers float gently about within their rubber rings, and giant water lilies bloom from May to November. The turreted pavilion and wooden catwalks add more than a touch of fantasy here.

**Below:** *Hévíz spa is situated by Europe's largest thermal lake.*

**Esztergom**
**Location:** Map D–A1
**Distance from**
**Budapest:** 45km
(30 miles)

**Eger**
**Location:** Map F–F1
**Distance from**
**Budapest:** 128km
(80 miles)

## Esztergom

You see the green dome of Esztergom's neo-Classical **Basilica** towering above the city long before you reach it. The seat of Catholicism in Hungary, it occupies the site where Esztergom-born King Stephen I was crowned on Christmas Day 1000. Its dimensions are vast – 118m (387ft) by 40m (131ft), surmounted by a 72m (236ft) high dome.

The basilica's originators in 1822 were Pál Kühneland and János Packh; József Hild, designer of Eger's cathedral, was involved in its completion by 1869. The cathedral had been consecrated 13 years before, with a Mass composed by Liszt. Don't miss the striking copy of Titian's *Assumption* over the main alter. The Bakócz Chapel in red and white marble is to the left of the entrance and the basilica's treasury to the right. Climb to the bell tower and to the cupola for superb views of the city.

Immediately south of the basilica – on the site of the Roman fortress of Solva Mansio – is the reconstructed former **Royal Palace**, originally built by Béla III and used by Hungarian monarchs for 300 years until capital status switched to Buda. It was subsequently the archbishop's seat until its destruction by the Turks, and it now houses the **Castle Museum** in a number of well-restored rooms.

**Opposite:** *Eger's castle stands proud above this appealing city.*
**Below:** *Esztergom Basilica is the seat of Catholicism in Hungary.*

## Eger

Eger is known for its Baroque architecture, the castle, and Egri Bikavér, a tipple that's known as Bull's Blood.

Historically, Eger's greatest moment came in 1552, when a mere 2000 Hungarian militia successfully defended the castle against some 40,000 Turks; legend has it that the women played their part by dousing the invaders with hot soup. In 1596, the Turks returned to take the city and stayed for 100 years; the **minaret** that rises above Eger's rooftops is their legacy (climb its 100 steps for a city overview). Within the castle are the remains of the 12th-century St John's Cathedral.

**Eger Cathedral**, completed in 1836, is Hungary's second largest church after the Esztergom basilica and bears a strong resemblance to it – both neo-Classical buildings were designed by József Hild. Its organ is the largest in the land. Next to it, the rambling Baroque **Archbishop's Palace** has been home to Eger's bishops for 250 years. The late 18th-century **Lyceum** – now a teachers' training college – has a couple of real gems in its first-floor Diocesan Library and sixth-floor observatory, complete with a 200-year-old camera obscura.

Other Eger highlights are the Cistercian Church (1743), the twin-towered Baroque Minorite Church (1773) and the Franciscan Church (1755) and County Hall, with its wrought-iron work by Henrik Fazola.

### The Lippizaners
The white Lippizaner horses commonly associated with the Spanish Riding School in Vienna and which take their name from the stud at Lipica in Slovenia are also bred at **Szilvásvárad**, 27km (17 miles) north of Eger in northern Hungary. There are around 250 horses here, the descendants of Arabian, Spanish and Berber breeds. As well as performing at dressage events, they have a role as carriage horses. Smallish in build, the Lippizaners are characterized by their long backs and short, thick necks.

**Above:** *Esterházy Palace is the finest Baroque mansion in Hungary.*

### Esterházy Palace

Some 27km (16 miles) east of Sopron, Fertőd boasts Hungary's most beautiful Baroque mansion. The 126-room Esterházy Palace, labelled the 'Hungarian Versailles', was started in 1720 and took 46 years to complete for the country's richest aristocratic family. In its glory years during the latter part of the 18th century, and with **Joseph Haydn** as court composer, the palace cultivated a reputation for its sumptuous balls and social gatherings. But it fell into decline in the 1800s and only after World War II, when it served as a hospital, was restoration begun seriously. A tour of the palace takes in two dozen or so rooms; on summer weekends, concerts are staged here.

## Sopron

Sopron has more historical monuments than any Hungarian town and Belváros (the inner town) is most rewarding.

The centre point of Sopron is Fő tér, beneath the 60m (196ft) **fire tower;** climb it for a fine view. By the tower, **Loyalty Gate** (1922) acknowledges the Sopron citizens' decision to choose Hungarian status after the Trianon Treaty of 1920; the Latin phrase *Civitas Fidelissima* on Sopron's coat of arms means 'most loyal citizenry'.

The Baroque **Holy Trinity Column** on Fő tér was completed in 1701. Behind it stands the **Goat Church**, named after the heraldic identity of its main benefactor. In a Gothic building next door is a **Pharmacy Museum.**

Along the square's northern side are three museums. **Fabricius House**, a museum of 17th- and 18th-century Sopron domestic life, is furnished accordingly; Renaissance **Storno House** (1417) contains the worthwhile private art collection of the Storno dynasty; and the **General's House** was the Mayor's residence in the 17th century.

From Fő tér, Templom utca and Új utca are parallel streets leading south. Templom utca contains more museums – the **Mining Museum** in a former Esterházy mansion at No. 2, the **Forestry Museum** at No. 4, and the **Lutheran Museum** in the priests' seminary at No. 12, next to the Lutheran Church from 1782. On Új utca, a former Jewish street, are two 14th-century **synagogues**.

## Kecskemét

The centre of Kecskemét is based on two large squares, Szabadság tér and Kossuth tér, which join in a single expanse of inner-city greenery. On the north side of Szabadság tér you can't miss the distinctive Cifrapalota (**Ornamental Palace**), a remarkable piece of Art Nouveau complete with glazed majolica tiles built in 1902. It now houses the **Kecskemét Gallery**, and upstairs is a fine tile-decorated hall that was once a casino.

Facing the square across Rákóczi utca is the white Moorish-Romantic-style former Synagogue, completed in 1871; it is now the **House of Science and Technology** exhibition venue. On the east side of the square opposite the Cifrapalota is the **New College**, built in the Gothic style of Transylvania (1912), which now houses the Ecclesiastical Art Collection.

The **Calvinist Church** on the east side of Kossuth tér is from the 17th century; the **Franciscan Church** just south of it has 13th-century origins. Behind the church, the **Kodály Institute** occupies the Baroque former Franciscan monastery. The square's south side is taken up by Ödön Lechner's pink **Town Hall** (1893) and the Baroque **Catholic Great Church** (1806).

Museums in Kecskemét include the **Photography Museum** (in Bajcsy-Zsilinszky utca) with some 300,000 photos; the **Naïve Art Museum** (in Gáspár András utca) and nearby **Toy Museum**, the **Hungarian Folk Craft Museum** (Serfőző utca), and the **Musical Instrument Museum** (Zimay utca).

> **Sopron**
> **Location:** Map F–A1
> **Distance from Budapest:** 217km
> (135 miles)
>
> **Kecskemét**
> **Location:** Map F–E3
> **Distance from Budapest:** 85km
> (53 miles)

**Below:** *The stately Katona Theatre in Kecskemét pays tribute to the town's romantic playwright.*

**Above:** *Traffic swarms over the Elizabeth Bridge between Pest and Buda.*

## Tourist Information

The **Hungarian National Tourist Office** is represented abroad in the UK (London), the USA (New York), Japan (Tokyo) and throughout Europe. The UK address is ⊠ 46 Eaton Place, London SW1X 8AL, ☎ 020 7823 1032, ℻ 020 7823 1459, ✆ info@goto hungary.co.uk 🖳 www.goto hungary.co.uk In Hungary, **Tour-** **inform** is at ⊠ Sütő utca 2, Deák tér, 1052 Budapest, ☎ 1 438 8080, ℻ 488 8661. It provides tourist information in English, Hungarian, German, French, Italian and Russian (🕘 open 08:00–20:00). Other Tourinform offices in Budapest are at: ⊠ Nyugati (Western) Railway Station, Main Hall by platform 10, ☎ 1 302 8580; ⊠ Liszt Ferenc tér 11, ☎ 322 4098 (Pest VI); ⊠ Szentháromság tér in the Castle District, ☎ 488 0475 (Buda I); ⊠ Városház utca 7, ☎ 428 0377; and at ⊠ Ferihegy Airport. You can also call the Budapest Tourism Office on ☎ 0036 1 266 0482, ℻ 0036 1 266 7477.

## Embassies and Consulates

American Embassy, ⊠ Szabadság tér 12, ☎ 1 475 4400 (Pest V). Australian Embassy, ⊠ Királyhágó tér 8–9, ☎ 1 457 9777 (Buda XII).

British Embassy,
✉ Harmincad utca 6,
☎ 1 266 2888 (Pest V).
Canadian Embassy,
✉ Ganz utca 12–14,
☎ 1 392 3360 (Buda II).
South African
Embassy, ✉ Gárdonyi
Géza út 17, ☎ 1 392
0999 (Buda II).

## Entry Requirements

Nationals of most
European countries,
including the UK, and
the USA, Canada,
Australia and New
Zealand need only a
valid passport to stay
for up to 90 days.
Citizens of South
Africa will need a visa.

## Customs

The duty-free
allowance for goods
imported into
Hungary is 200 ciga-
rettes (or 100 cigars or
250g of tobacco), a
litre of spirits, a litre
of wine, five litres of
beer and gifts to the
value of Fts 29,500.

## Health
## Requirements

No vaccinations are
required to enter
Hungary. Free or
reduced-cost emer-
gency health treat-
ment is available to
British, Scandinavian
and most east
European visitors.
However, all visitors
are advised to arrange
their own comprehen-
sive travel and medical
insurance. Keep
receipts and invoices –
they will be needed if
you make a claim. For
emergency telephone
numbers, see Health
Services on page 91.

## Getting to Hungary

**By air:** International
flights to Hungary
land at Budapest's
Ferihegy Airport.
Malév Hungarian
Airlines and British
Airways operate at
least one flight
daily from London
Heathrow; Malév also
flies from London
Gatwick, and there
are low-cost airline
options. You can reach
Hungary by air from
most major European
cities, while Malév also
flies direct from New
York and Toronto.

From the airport, a
taxi or airport minibus
(☎ 296 8555) will get
you to the city centre.
Or you can use public
transport – the bus
marked *reptér-busz*
from outside the
airport's arrivals hall,
changing to the blue
metro line at the
Kőbánya-Kispest
terminus.

**By road:** Hungary is
developing a motor-
way network with
Budapest at its hub.
The M1 motorway
enters the country
from Vienna, linking
with the M0 ring road
around Budapest, the
M7 from Lake Balaton,
M5 from the south
and M3 from the east
of the country.

To drive in Hungary, or
to hire a car, you need
a valid national driv-
ing licence; you must
also be able to show
your car registration
document and have a
country sticker. Avoid
drinking *any* alcohol
before driving – even
the smallest amount
of alcohol in the
bloodstream is

enough to get you convicted. Use dimmed headlights outside built-up areas, even during daylight hours. Seat belts must be worn in the front of the car (and in the back outside built-up areas); children under 12 are not allowed to travel in the front seats. Driving in Hungary, like the rest of continental Europe, is on the right.

**By rail:** You can easily reach Hungary by international train from the capitals of neighbouring countries – Vienna (Austria) is 3 hours away, Prague (Czech Republic) 7½ hours and Bratislava (Slovakia) 2 hours 40 minutes. Most international trains arrive in Budapest at the Keleti (Eastern) station.

**By bus:** Long-distance buses operate to Hungary from the rest of Europe. Eurolines operates a year-round service to Budapest from London. Hungarian bus com-

pany Volánbusz operates services from a total of 17 European countries; they arrive in Budapest at Volánbusz coach station in Erzsébet tér.

**By river:** A hydrofoil service operates daily from Apr to the end of Oct on the Danube from Vienna to Budapest via Bratislava. The 282km (175-mile) Vienna-Budapest journey takes 5½ hours. The return trip upriver takes 6 hours and 20 minutes.

## What to Pack

Remember that Hungary experiences a continental climate, with hot summers and cold winters. From Jun to Sep you need only light clothing – take beachwear if you intend spending time stretched out in the sun by Lake Balaton. In late spring and autumn, a fold-up umbrella will deal with the odd shower; pack warmer clothes for the evenings. In winter go prepared

for severe chill, though in equal proportions you may enjoy crisp sunny days or suffer damp and cloudy conditions.

## Money Matters

**Currency:** The unit of currency in Hungary is the forint (abbreviated Huf or Ft). Banknotes are 200, 500, 1000, 2000, 5000, 10,000 and 20,000 forints; coins are 1, 2, 5, 10, 20, 50 and 100 forints. Note that some hotels price their rates in Euro, owing to the changing value of the forint.

**Currency exchange:** Money and travellers' cheques can be exchanged at banks, exchange bureaux and hotels, though banks offer the best rate. Automatic teller machines (ATMs) are found throughout the country and are by far the easiest way to top up your cash reserves. Forget the street-corner black market – it's illegal, there's little dvantage to be ained and you may well be ripped off. If ou have forints left ver at the end of our visit they can e reconverted, but ou will need to produce the original exchange receipt.

**Credit cards:** The leading credit cards – Visa, American Express and MasterCard – are accepted at most hotels, restaurants, shops and petrol stations. But carry cash as well and be prepared to use it in museums, galleries and supermarkets and for bus and train travel.

**Tipping:** The custom in Hungarian restaurants is to round up the bill or to add 10 per cent; sometimes, the bill will include a 10 per cent service charge. Give the tip when the bill arrives and tell the waiter how much, rather than leave the coins on the table. Taxi drivers, hairdressers, beauticians and petrol station attendants are

also tipped as a matter of routine.

**Taxes:** Sales tax (ÁFA) of between 15 and 25 per cent is usually included in the cost of a purchase, but check before you buy. For purchases of 25,000 forints or more, you can claim back the tax before leaving the country. For further advice, contact Europe Tax Free Shopping Hungary at ⊠ Bég utca 3–5 (Buda II), ☎ 1 212 4906.

## Accommodation

Visitors to Hungary will find all levels of accommodation, from basic youth hostels and rooms in private homes to full-service five-star hotels. Cities and towns have well-priced mid-range hotels suitable for touring visitors; if you're in Budapest with money to spare you might splash out on a deluxe night or two. In rural areas, there are pensions and inns offering simple accommodation.

**Useful Phrases**

How are you?
• *Hogy van?*
Do you speak English?
• *Beszél angolul?*
I don't speak Hungarian • *Nem tudok magyarul*
What is your name?
• *Mi a neve?*
My name is …
• *A nevem …*
How much is this?
• *Mennyibe kerül?*
I would like …
• *Kérek szépen …*
The bill, please
• *Kérem a számlát*
What is the time?
• *Hány óra?*
Good day • *Jó napot*
Good morning
• *Jó reggelt*
Good evening
• *Jó estét*
Goodnight
• *Jó éjszakát*
Goodbye • *Viszlát*
Yes/No • *Igen/Nem*
Please/thank you
• *Kérem/Köszönöm*
Sorry • *Bocsánat*
Left/Right • *Bal/Jobb*

## Useful Phrases
airport • *repülőtér*
alley • *fasor, köz*
arrival • *érkezés*
avenue • *út, útja*
boat • *hajó*
boulevard • *körút*
bridge • *híd*
bus • *busz*
café • *kávéház*
circle • *köröndi*
closed • *zárva*
departure • *indulás*
embankment • *rakpart*
entrance • *bejárat*
exit • *kijárat*
highway • *autópálya*
hill • *hegy*
island • *sziget*
ladies' room • *nők, hölgyek*
men's room • *férfiak, urak*
open • *nyitva*
platform • *peron*
prohibited • *tilos*
restaurant • *étterem*
square • *tér, tere*
station • *állomás*
street • *utca*
train • *vonat*

## Language
Hungarian is a difficult language to learn, so any attempt to speak it is well received. Even *köszönöm* (thank you) in appreciation of services rendered is better than nothing. In Budapest, you will get by with German, while English may be understood in hotels and restaurants, but in provincial Hungary the vast majority of people speak only Hungarian.

Tourinform offices can provide information on where to stay in their locality. Leading Hungarian hotel group Danubius Hotels has a UK office, through which reservations can be made, at ✉ CP House, Otterspool Way, Watford, Herts WD25 8JP, ☎ 01923 650 290, ℻ 01923 650 268.

## Eating Out

Hungary prides itself on its cuisine, and with good reason. You will never have trouble finding somewhere warm and inviting to eat – and with prices extremely affordable by western European standards, you might find yourself not even bothering to look at the price before ordering. In Budapest, you can seek out every kind of ethnic eatery – from Mexican to Mongolian, Greek to Korean. Restaurants serving traditional Hungarian fare can be found in abun-

dance throughout the country, with a range of Hungary's fine quality wines to accompany your meal.

## Transport

Hungary's rail network radiates from Budapest, with trains departing from one of three termini – Keleti, the eastern station; Nyugati, the western station; and Déli, across the river in Buda. Points served from Keleti include Békéscsaba, Eger, Győr, Keszthely, Lake Balaton, Miskolc, Sopron, Szolnok and Szombathely; from Nyugati, trains run to Debrecen, Kecskemét, Szeged and Záhony; from Déli there are departures for Kaposvár and Pécs. There are Hungarian Flexipass rail passes for tourists and a Lake Balaton day ticket giving unlimited travel around the lake. Information on domestic rail services is available on ☎ 1 461 5400.

Hungary also boasts 16 narrow-gauge railways, scattered throughout the country and operating along a total 380km (236 miles) of track. Steam-hauled 'nostalgia' trains run from Keszthely to Badacsony and from Budapest's Nyugati station to Szob on the Danube Bend in summer. For information, ☎ 1 428 0180.

Within Budapest, the three underground railway lines of the Metro converge at Deák tér, on the Pest side of the river. Trains run at intervals of up to 12 minutes – every two minutes in the rush hour – ☺ 04:30 until 23:10. The HÉV suburban railway has four lines, three on the Pest side of the city and the fourth serving Óbuda, Aquincum and Szentendre on the Danube Bend.

**Buses:** Volánbusz, the national Hungarian bus operator, runs 108 services throughout the country, many of them radiating from Budapest's two coach hubs – Erzsébet tér bus station and the Népstadion bus station. For information on bus services within Hungary, call the Volánbusz central information desk, ☎ 1 382 0888; or ☎ 1 329 1450 (Árpád híd bus station, for Danube Bend).

In Budapest, trams and buses offer a comprehensive service around the city. Trolleybuses run mainly to the north and east of downtown Pest. Buses run every 10–20 minutes from ☺ 05:00 until 23:00 throughout the city and are useful in Buda's hilly areas. Night buses operate on 17 routes and carry an 'É' suffix.

**Road:** Hungary's four motorways are the M1 towards Vienna, the M3 towards Debrecen, the M5 to the south and the M7 to Lake Balaton. They radiate from Budapest and require a vignette motorway sticker, available at border crossings and petrol stations. The roads are generally good, well signposted and relatively free of traffic; in northern Hungary and on the Great Plain you could drive for miles without seeing another vehicle. The speed limit for cars is 130 km/h (81 mph) on motorways, 100 km/h (60 mph) on dual carriageways, 90 km/h (56 mph) on single carriageways and 50 km/h (30 mph) in built-up areas.

**Car rental:** The leading international car-rental companies are represented in Hungary, along with local firms. Companies include Avis, Budget and Hertz, all with rental desks at Budapest's Ferihegy airport.

## Business Hours

Banks are open from ☺ 08:00 until 14:00 from Monday to Thursday, occasionally

**Public Holidays**
**1 January** • New Year's Day
**15 March** • Anniversary of the 1848 Revolution
**March/April** • Easter Sunday and Monday
**1 May** • Labour Day
**June** • Whit Sunday and Monday
**20 August** • St Stephen's Day (founding of the state)
**23 October** • Republic Day (anniversary of the 1956 Revolution)
**25–26 December** • Christmas

**Below:** *An ornate postbox in central Budapest.*

later, and ☺ 08:00 until 13:00 on Friday; they are closed on Saturday and Sunday. In Budapest, some *bureaux de change* are open during weekends.

Principal post offices open ☺ 08:00 until 18:00 or 19:00 Monday to Friday and until 13:00 on Saturday; minor post offices close at 15:30 and don't open at weekends.

Shopping hours roughly correspond to those of other central European towns and cities. Most super-markets are open ☺ 09:00 until 19:00 Monday to Friday; 07:00 until 13:00 on Saturday, with some opening on Sunday. The word 'nonstop' translates as being open 24 hours, whether convenience grocery store or all-night café. Other shops and department stores tend to open ☺ 10:00 until 18:00 Monday to Friday and 09:00 until 13:00 Saturday. Some department stores keep longer hours and in Budapest, large shopping centres like the Westend City Center by the Western station remain open until late at weekends. Museums are generally open ☺ 10:00 until 18:00 from Tue to Sun between Apr and Oct (10:00 until 16:00 in winter), but close on Mon.

**Time Difference**
Hungary is on Central European Time, one hour ahead of GMT i▮

winter and two hours ahead in summer (from the last Sunday in March until the last Sunday in October). The 24-hour clock is widely used.

## Communications

International telephone calls can be made from public call boxes – dial ☎ 00, wait for the dialling tone and then dial the country code, area code and the number required. Public phone boxes with a red target and black-and-white arrow on the door display a call-back number, which you can give to the person you are calling – the dialling code for Hungary is ☎ 0036. Phone numbers in Budapest are seven-digit (area code 1); others have eight digits, including the two-digit area code. Phone cards of 50 and 120 units can be bought in post offices, newsagents or from tobacconists.

## Electricity

In Hungary the power supply is 220 volts, 50 cycles. Sockets are two-pin and an adaptor is needed for British, American and Australian appliances.

## Weights and Measures

Hungary uses the metric system for all measurements.

## Health Services

**American Clinic,** ✉ Hattyú utca 14, Budapest I, ☎ 224 9090 (⊕ 24-hour emergency service).
**Falck SOS Hungary,** ✉ Kapy utca 49, Budapest II, ☎ 200 0100 (⊕ 24-hour outpatient service).
**Dental emergencies** (⊕ 24 hours) in Budapest, ☎ 342 6972, 322 0602 and 329 0200.
**Pharmacies** (⊕ 24 hours) in Budapest, ☎ 311 4439, 314 3693 and 355 4691.

## Personal Safety

Hungary is no less safe than the majority of other European countries and there is little risk to tourists. Nevertheless visitors should always be on their guard against petty theft, which does occur from time to time – entrust your valuables to a hotel safe rather than carrying them with you and beware of pickpockets. In Budapest, it's wise to steer clear of the area between Rákóczi tér, the red light district, and the Keleti railway terminus, especially at night.

## Emergencies

**Ambulance,** ☎ 104 (in English, ☎1 311 1666).
**Police,** ☎ 107.
**Fire,** ☎ 105.
**Autoclub Emergency** (in English), ☎ 188.
**Other useful numbers:**
Directory enquiries, ☎ 198 (domestic), ☎ 199 (international). Hungarian Disabled Association (MEOSZ), ☎ 1 388 2387/5529 (⊕ 08:00–16:00 weekdays).

# INDEX OF SIGHTS

# General Index

# GENERAL INDEX

# General Index